THE FOURTH FACTOR

THE FOURTH FACTOR

Managing Corporate Culture

Linda Ford

dog ear
PUBLISHING

First published by Dog Ear Publishing
4010 W. 86th Street, Ste H
Indianapolis, IN 46268
www.dogearpublishing.net

dog ear
PUBLISHING

ISBN: 978-159858-429-5

This book is printed on acid-free paper.

Printed in the United States of America

ADVANCE PRAISE FOR *THE FOURTH FACTOR*

"Culture matters. What Ford calls the fourth factor is at least as important as products, customers, and cash in getting results and generating shareholder value. Any executive who wants to successfully manage culture should heed the practical advice Ford provides."

Jonathan Schwartz,
CEO, Sun Microsystems, Inc.

"My personal attention to culture, what Ford calls the fourth factor, has been important in building 1-800-GOT-JUNK? into an internationally recognized brand. Ford has done a great job of creating a book that allows leaders at all levels of the organization to lead more effectively by understanding and managing culture. A must read for executives!"

Brian Scudamore
Founder and CEO, 1-800-GOT-JUNK?

"Ford's wonderful new book on the Gorilla of corporate culture is brilliantly practical, carefully thought out, and clearly written. To mix metaphors, the blind men (and women) can finally begin to see the sides of the elephant when it comes to culture."

Michele Bolton
Author of The Third Shift

"This is an important work on a significant subject for serious leaders who want to grow extraordinary organizations. Dr. Ford elaborates with clarity and wisdom about the power of culture in any environment."

Nido R. Qubein
Chairman, Great Harvest Bread Company
President, High Point University

"Linda Ford has finally provided an answer to every CEO's question of "We've tried everything, and the problem persists. What's wrong?' Read *The Fourth Factor*, and you'll pick up that missing organizational link."

George W. Kessinger
CEO, Goodwill Industries International

"CEOs, boards of directors, and Wall Street analysts should all be paying attention to *The Fourth Factor*. Ford's view that leaders who don't manage culture can't successfully manage products, customers, and cash is dead-on. Buyouts, mergers, and other financial deals often fail to produce shareholder value because the leaders don't understand culture. Anyone who cares about building shareholder value should read this book."

Ross Garber
Cofounder, Vignette Corporation

"Ford really nailed the importance of harnessing organizational culture. Her practical explanation of how culture works is right on target and provides actionable insights for managers and human resource professionals alike. The examples and stories will help our management team see themselves in the role of culture leaders. This is an important addition to every leader's bookshelf."

Kay Stroman,
Vice president, Human Resources, Grande Communication, Inc.

"I'm giving every leader in my portfolio a copy of this book. It's full of nuggets of wisdom aptly backed by real-life stories. Dr. Ford is savvy and street-smart with a deep foundation of knowledge. She speaks my language and understands my business problems."

Ed Perry
General Partner, Murphree Venture Partners

"A very helpful, provocative book, which should be read by anyone wanting to bring a business into higher-level performance. Ford's enthusiasm and brilliant use of metaphor as well as very real examples provide interest as well as solid information."

Marjorie R. Barlow, PhD
Author of The Possible Woman

"Linda Ford delivers a message in her book that CEOs ignore at their own peril: an organization's culture can and should be managed just like any other strategic asset. Linda provides real-world examples and real-world advice that is actionable—the rest is up to us."

Bill Daniel
CEO, Surgient, Inc.

"Ford arms the individual with a manifesto on how to unleash employees' creativity and energy. This book explains how you, as an individual, can affect change in an organization, taking culture into account. This an absolutely great read."

Ed Anderson,
Senior Vice President, Sales and Business Development, Digital
Standard, Inc.

"Ford's gorilla metaphor for organizational culture provides an image that anyone at any level of the organization can understand. And the tools to apply this knowledge are all right along side the gorilla in her book."

Steve Harper
Author of The Ripple Effect

"*The Fourth Factor* offers our employees a means of exploring their personal views and attitudes about beliefs and behaviors that will influence the success of our culture building and sustaining efforts. Thank you for providing a practical text written for leaders, trainers, and our producers and service providers."

Jim Ronay
EH Systems

CONTENTS

ACKNOWLEDGMENTS

It takes a village to raise a child. This book is no different than any other child. It was raised with the caring support of a whole village of friends and colleagues. My gratitude to all of you is deep and enduring.

Pat Kirkland: From the intellectual structure of the ideas to the smallest detail of language, you've been right there with me. You've celebrated my successes with me and put me back together when life wasn't turning out right, all with an abiding faith in me that made all the difference.

Kathy Long: From the time we first met at Fielding as we were just beginning our PhD journeys, we've been joined at the hip intellectually. You loaned me your right brain to balance out my left brain and you kept me from going nuts.

Pat Marriott: Ten years before it was time for me to write this book, you were the first who said, "You should write a book about this stuff!" When I finally wrote, you tirelessly edited both the book and the many articles and other bits. Piggies or no, it's finally here.

Dale Weisman: As a "real" writer, you were brutally honest about my writing and it made a huge difference. Because you followed your criticisms with a hug and a glass of wine, I never cried for too long.

Jeff Browning: You were the last to say, "You should write a book." By giving me the first working title and your vote of confidence, you launched the serious writing phase.

Will McWhinney, Charlie Seashore, and Jeremy Shapiro: During my years as a Fielding student and beyond, each of you expanded my intellectual horizons and enlarged my heart immeasurably. You taught me to swim in the deep end, where all the interesting things happen.

Sam Horn: You gave my material that extra sizzle it needed and helped me see what I was missing.

My mom, LaNelle Ford, and my sister, Kathryn Ford: Obviously, you've been there since the beginning, literally. Both of you have shown me that it's never too late to make your dreams come true. You've inspired and supported me all along the way.

My dad, Dennis Ford: Your mind and your work formed the early ground from which my later professional work emerged. I only wish I had gotten this done before you passed on so you could have enjoyed it with me.

Dee Alcott, Ross Garber, Ed Perry, Jerry Davis, Bill Daniel, and all the other dedicated executives who have allowed me to work with you to build your organizations: In your drive for excellence, you helped me reach beyond what I knew to learn along with you. You stretched my thinking and demanded my best work. This book wouldn't exist without you.

Allison Allen, Ed Anderson, Marj Barlow, Susan Brooks, Charlyn Daugherty, Sam Decker, Chris Douglas, Peter Finkelstein, Glen Powell, Nido Qubein, Prince Rahman, Jim Ronay, Tom Ryan: Thank you all for reading the manuscript in its early forms and providing your honest comments and suggestions. I appreciate your friendship.

Thank you all from the bottom of my heart.

PREFACE

This book will help you if you:

- Think your organization can achieve greater results but haven't been able to attain those results yet
- Have been frustrated by your inability to drive change in your organization
- Are tired of wasting time on office politics
- Want work to be more fulfilling for you and your employees
- Are concerned about your organization's ability to attract and retain topnotch people as the talent shortage gets more severe.

In short, if you are a leader in an organization or if you want to be more successful, this book is for you.

Although organizational culture is a significant force in your organization, it is invisible. There's nothing you can point to as you walk down the hall and say, "There it is. That's the culture." That makes it hard to talk about. This book can help you start a conversation about culture and change with your team.

You'll often hear that culture change has to start at the top. My perspective is somewhat different. Everyone can be a leader. As a leader, your actions affect the culture in your organization. Granted the CEO's actions have a broader impact than a frontline manager's actions. Whatever your position in the organization, you can use your leadership to shape the organization in positive ways. Use the principles in this book to make your organization a better place to work and a more successful organization. Don't wait until "they" solve the problems. Step up to the challenge and be a leader.

If you are the CEO, the notion that everyone can lead by managing the culture has several advantages over the top-down model. It creates an attitude of ownership for the success of the business throughout your organization. By partnering with willing leaders wherever you find them, you will develop the leadership capacity of your organization. Encouraging leadership everywhere will make change easier, whether it's top down or not.

What's Different About This Book

This isn't the first book to tackle the topic of organizational culture, and it won't be the last. There are four significant things that are different about this book.

Accessible explanations of how culture works: Most of the solid explanations of how culture actually works—where that 800-Pound Gorilla gets its phenomenal power—are buried in academic literature. Once you understand how culture actually works, you'll learn how to use that knowledge to manage culture in your organization.

From abstractions to nuts and bolts behaviors: When we talk about the key directives that drive your culture, we won't stop with high-level principles. I'll take you into the specifics of the behaviors that reflect these directives. Without that, any set of principles or directives can end up being just another set of pretty words.

Building a consistent culture with an overlay of diversity: Your corporate culture must thrive in a multicultural context. How do you create a consistent culture within your organization while taking the diversity of that multicultural context into account? In each chapter outlining a Gorilla directive, we'll look at the multicultural challenges and opportunities relevant to that directive.

Systemic approach: Organizational change isn't achieved through a set of independent ideas. It's an integrated, systemic approach. Too often, the practical business books take a very simplified, linear approach, leaving the systemic view to the academics. My approach is both systemic and practical.

This book draws on real "in the trenches" business experience along with powerful theories and models. The examples and stories are all real events from real organizations, drawn from my three decades of business experiences. The principles in this book represent an integration of what I've learned in helping more than one hundred organizations create positive change during the past fifteen years of consulting. To make the examples more concise and relevant, I've sometimes blended multiple incidents into one story to emphasize the point. In most cases, I've disguised the identities of both people and organizations.

Using This Book

Part One explains how culture actually works and how you can manage it. Chapter 1 provides a framework for understanding what culture is and how it functions. Chapter 2 reveals the principles of how the Gorilla's Guide supports and reinforces the culture and then explores the multi-track recording format used to create and update the Gorilla's Guide. You must understand this to successfully manage culture.

Part Two is dedicated to the six directives that must be embedded in your culture if you want your organization to achieve its full potential for success. These directives are the essential ingredients of a culture that drives success. Chapters 3 through 8 each cover one directive. The directive is translated to specific key behaviors and illustrated with examples from a variety of organizations. Each chapter addresses the challenges of working with organizational culture in a multicultural context, as well as other issues specific to that directive.

In Part Three, you'll learn how to lead your organization in integrating these directives into your culture. Chapters 9 through 12 reveal the three essential leadership actions of managing culture. After you've mastered that, the conclusion will wrap it all up for you.

You can read the book front to back or browse at random. It's all an integrated system, so dividing topics into chapters is simply an accommodation to the linear structure of a book. Read what catches your fancy. However, Chapter 2 is central to the logic of the book. If you skip around and find you are confused, go back and read that chapter.

Please, write all over this book if you disagree with what I've said, if the way I translate a directive into behaviors is different than how it would work in your organization, or when ideas for implementing these principles in your own organization occur to you.

Talk with other members of your team about the material. Share your margin notes with them. The more actively you engage with this material, the more you will move from studying the Gorilla to taming it.

For further resources, please visit www.FourthFactorOnline.com. And I'd love to hear about your ideas, additions, changes, and disagreements. Please e-mail me at Gorilla@FordBusinessConsulting.com.

I sincerely hope you will use this book to create a culture that supports your organization's success!

PART ONE

YOUR GORILLA

In the late 1980s, I was the product manager for a large data storage product at Tandem Computers. Actually, I was the hardware product manager. There was also a separate software product manager. I reported to Larry, the vice president of hardware. The software product manager reported to the vice president of software. We didn't share a common boss until we got all the way up to the CEO. Of course, my hardware product required the right software functionality to meet the customers' needs. Hardware by itself was useless. I worked hard to create a partnership with my counterpart in the software organization. But he had his own boss, goals, and meetings to worry about, and they weren't aligned with mine. I was frustrated!

One day, I marched into Larry's office and asked if we couldn't do something about this absurd structure. His answer was basically a patient version of "No, that's just the way it is." At that moment, my career direction changed.

That's when I realized the importance of the fourth factor. Managers tend to keep their eye on three critical success factors: products, customers, and cash. But the fourth factor—culture—can undermine anything you try to do with the first three. Beginning that day in Larry's office, I stopped focusing on technology and started focusing on culture.

Organizational culture is the 800-Pound Gorilla in your organization. Do you know what the gorilla has for lunch? Anything it wants! That's exactly what corporate culture is doing in your organization. It does anything it wants, whether it helps you succeed or not.

Back to the story. As luck would have it, my son, then six years old, and I had recently watched *Gorillas in the Mist*, based on Dian Fossey's up-close and personal work with mountain gorillas in Rwanda. I was struck by how human the gorillas seemed. There is so much about these magnificent creatures that is so very much like us. When I later read Fossey's book, on which the movie was based, I found the connections even more powerful. In Fossey's description of the gorilla groups' behavior and relationships, I saw all of those staff meetings, product meetings, and customer briefings in a totally new light.

Now you know the origin of this book's gorilla theme. To introduce each chapter, I've borrowed a vignette from Fossey's book. You can see for yourself whether there are similarities between the mountain gorillas' behavior and your organization's culture. I'm not saying you work with a bunch of apes. There are just some striking similarities in behavior.

Now you also know why I had to write this book. Too many organizations are suffering because they are ignoring the fourth factor—culture—and focusing all their attention on products, customers, and finances.

Most executives hate dealing with culture because it's invisible. They don't know how to manage or measure it, let alone change it. Using the metaphor of culture as an 800-pound gorilla, this book reveals the workings of culture in a practical, accessible way and shows you how to take charge of your destiny by managing your culture. We're going to take culture from a soft, nebulous concept that can't be managed to a strategic asset that must be managed.

Simply, culture is "how things are done around here." It's the one thing that shapes everything else. It creates your successes—and your failures. Culture is at least partially to blame for large-scale disasters such as the British Petroleum Arctic pipeline leak, the explosion of the *Challenger* space shuttle, and the rampant corruption at Enron.

Culture is also central to frustrations you face every day in your business, including the inability to change strategic directions more quickly than your competition, a failed merger or joint venture, or the isolation of functional silos in the organization. All of these frustrations and disasters can be attributed, at least partially, to organizational culture.

Many leaders also credit organizational culture as the driving force behind significant organizational accomplishments. Brian Scudamore founded 1-800-GOT-JUNK? with a $700 investment in a used pickup. Scudamore has worked hard to create a culture that helps people succeed and love their work. That's helped him parlay his $700 investment into an international organization with $160 million in annual revenues. As the company grew, he came to believe more strongly that "it's all about people." As Scudamore told me, "When you get everyone aligned with the vision and hold the team accountable for the culture, it all comes together, and the business hums."

Scudamore is not alone in that belief. Several years ago, the founder of another company told me simply, "Culture makes the impossible possible."

Even though I had my frustrations at Tandem, the company's culture had some remarkably good qualities. We worked hard, played hard, and laughed a lot. There was a level of trust in employees that was uncommon in the 1980s. All of these qualities made Tandem a fun place to work and contributed to the organization's success. There were also dysfunctional aspects of the culture, including the hard line between hardware and software.

Most organizational cultures have both positive and negative qualities. In that way, the gorilla is an apt metaphor. It can be angry and destructive, but it is also a gentle, intelligent creature.

A successful culture provides a competitive advantage that is virtually impossible to duplicate. This will be increasingly important as the global talent shortage becomes more severe. Statisticians estimate that, in 2008, approximately 12 million experienced workers will leave the workforce. Only 3.5 million new workers will enter the workforce. Your organization needs to be able to attract and retain talent in that market. Managing culture is vital to your ability to do that.

Executives often turn to successful organizations that have a well-defined culture, like Southwest Airlines, to learn how to duplicate those cultures. However, they often walk away with bits and pieces, not realizing that the whole is much greater than the sum of the parts. In this book, we'll discuss culture as a system of interconnected ideas, beliefs, and behaviors that will make your organization more successful.

Which comes first? A change in the culture produces changes in behavior; a consistent change in behavior produces a change in culture. This is all part of the puzzle of managing and changing culture.

CHAPTER 1

ANYTHING IT WANTS!

It's a rainy day and the gorilla group has stopped for a rest period. As usual, each adult constructs a bathtub nest out of bushy branches in the clearing. These large, sturdy nests provide some measure of shelter and comfort during the downpour. However, Beethoven, the silverback alpha male, built a rather slipshod nest. As the rain became heavier, rather than rebuild the nest or suffer his discomfort, he marched over to one of the adult females and squeezed into her nest with her! Why should Beethoven suffer when the silverback can get Anything It Wants!

Gorillas in the Mist

Your organizational culture is just like Beethoven. It can make up its own rules, and you can't tell it what to do. Culture, the 800-Pound Gorilla, is simply "the way we do things around here." It's an all-pervasive environment that shapes individual expectations, actions, interpretations, and responses to events in a given organizational context. You don't have to see or understand it to be influenced by it. It affects everything you do (and everything your employees do) in your organization. You do have to understand it to successfully manage it and make it a strategic ally. You manage three critical success factors for your business: products, customers, and finances. The fourth factor—culture—impacts all of those.

When the Hewlett-Packard board asked for Carly Fiorina's resignation in February, 2004, the headlines generally labeled the situation as either execution problems or disagreements about strategy. Certainly, both areas of concern were legitimate, but I'll suggest a different perspective. Fiorina was a very "me" person in a very "we" culture. During a speech at Stanford in 2001, one journalist counted the number of times she said "I"—more than one hundred times. After her dismissal, the *Wall Street Journal* cited "acting like a rock star" as number one of Fiorina's "seven deadly sins." There are certainly many CEOs who could be accused of acting like rock stars or being too "me" focused. But at Hewlett-Packard, the corporate culture supports collaboration and teamwork, not rock stars. This perspective on the story suggests that Fiorina tangled with Hewlett-Packard's Gorilla and lost. As the Hewlett-Packard story unfolded in the years immediately following Fiorina's resignation, we continued to reinterpret what had happened. As with most large-scale change, it will be a long time before we fully understand all that was involved. But the role of culture is significant.

When new CEO Mike Ullman took over JCPenney in 2004, he set about changing its deeply entrenched culture. JCPenney's century-old culture was based on very specific and explicit messages right from the start. Ullman knew he was walking a tightrope. He was trying to make changes without destroying more than a century of corporate tradition. Recognizing his front-line store personnel are "the first customers we sell," Ullman brought about changes, including implementing a casual dress code, putting everyone on a first name basis, and instituting major management training initiatives. So far, Ullman seems to be succeeding. In January 2007, JCPenney posted its fifteenth consecutive quarter of sales gains along with a 33 percent year over year increase in earnings per share. It's still early, but Ullman is apparently successfully taming the JCPenney corporate culture Gorilla. And it's having a very positive impact on the bottom line.

Culture changes take a long time to unfold fully. But at this point, I'd say that Fiorina lost the battle at Hewlett-Packard in part partially because she ignored the culture. Ullman is working with the culture to create change and succeeding. He is in control of his destiny, influencing Penney's culture, not subject to its whims. In both situations, it's clear that the Gorilla throws its weight around—it cannot be ignored. Manage the culture effectively and you can control your destiny; ignore it at your own peril.

This is especially true if you are making a strategic shift in your business. Culture eats strategy for lunch every day. If you develop a new strategic initiative or direction and your culture doesn't support it, it will probably fail. Your best plans and programs will never be executed as you intended because the invisible messages that influence behavior are not aligned with your strategic initiatives. Like it or not, your culture is your silent partner. It is the critical link between strategy and execution.

Let's look at two contrasting news stories about well-known consumer technology companies to see the powerful influence that culture exerts on strategy and execution. In the summer of 2006, NPR's "Morning Edition" interviewed David Pogue, the technology columnist for the *New York Times*, about Microsoft's current challenges. He shared an anecdote that illuminates the culture at Microsoft.

Pogue had written a review of the latest Pocket PC by Microsoft, complaining about the user interface (as usual). A Microsoft public relations person called and asked if Pogue had any suggestions for the design team for the next Pocket PC, other than, as Pogue put it, "that interface stuff." As Pogue described it, his response was, "But, dude, it's about the interface stuff. There is nothing else in my view."

Clearly, both Pogue and the PR person knew Microsoft developers aren't generally focused on the user interface. In the Microsoft culture, user interface isn't a high priority. Whatever the design goals are for the next Pocket PC, the Gorilla at Microsoft knows "that interface stuff" isn't what the design team wants to talk about.

A couple weeks before that NPR story, a columnist at the *Wall Street Journal* pointed out that the rivals of Apple's iPod needed some "design mojo." In describing an Internet spoof, which Microsoft designers created, on what the iPod would look like if Microsoft designed it, he noted, "It's as if they know the sort of great design they ought to be doing, but are too smothered by a corporate culture to deliver it."

Can't you just imagine what that iPod designed by Microsoft looked like in the video spoof? Both columnists are telling us that it's not technology that separates Apple's notoriously user-friendly devices from Microsoft's geek-friendly products. It's the design culture. It's a culture with "design mojo" versus a culture that doesn't care about "that interface stuff." In both companies, the culture clearly cannot be ignored. You must manage your culture if you want to be in control of your own future.

Corn, Cars, and Concepts

If we go back about a century, we find ourselves in the agrarian age. We can fast-forward pretty quickly through the agrarian age and industrial age before entering today's economy. Some call it the "information age." Others call it the "experience economy." Still others call it the "age of imagination" or "age of ideas."

We've evolved from an economy based on corn, to one based on cars, and now to an economy based on concepts. From something you grow, to something you make, to something you think. What a shift! About the time we entered this new information age in the 1970s, corporate culture became a hot topic in the business press. With concepts on center stage, culture takes on a new level of importance.

If you want a place in today's economy, you must be adept at working with concepts: inventing, adapting, managing, cataloging, and implementing them. The more sophisticated or novel the concept, the more unique your role will be. As Daniel Pink pointed out in *A Whole New Mind*, with concepts we mostly use our right brain, but in the early stage of the information age, we used our left-brain skills. This is a shift in how we think.

The shift to concepts as the main ingredient of the economy also necessitates a shift in organizational culture. "Data driven" can be a good thing, but it's not the only thing. In an economy where concepts rule, we need to rediscover and communicate the stories, intuition, feelings, and wisdom that drive the concept economy. This shift isn't just about individual skills. It's also about how our organizations work.

All the things that influence how your employees think are significantly more important than they were in our parents' organizations. If you're still paying attention to the working environment instead of the thinking environment, your organization will get left behind. The raw material of concepts is thinking. One important source of fuel for thinking is conversation. The container for conversation is culture. That's why managing culture is so much more important in the twenty-first century.

Culture takes on additional importance when talent is in short supply. Statisticians tell us that we are heading into a talent shortage that will be more prolonged and deeper than what we experienced in the dot-com days. With an aging workforce and fewer people entering the workforce, organizations will need to improve their ability to retain top talent and create an environment for maximum productivity. Culture is a critical factor in both areas.

The principles that shape a concept-driven culture where great conversations breed innovative concepts aren't the same principles that drove success in the age of corn or cars. Production-centered work demands a culture focused on efficiency, volume, speed, and economies of scale. Concept-driven work demands relationships, innovation, and connections. Unfortunately, it doesn't do you any good to know those principles if you don't know what culture is made of, how it creates itself, and how to manage it. In these first two chapters, we'll look at how culture works before we discuss the key cultural directives you need for your organization to be successful.

The Gorilla's Guide

Your organizational culture contains and expresses your organization's worldview, philosophy, and attitudes. Along with the explicit statements, it includes all of the unspoken understandings about:

- How work is done
- How people interact
- How decisions are made

And many other small details of life in the organization.

Much of this is outside the awareness of the members of the organization. It's part of their tacit knowledge, that is, those things they know but don't know they know.

This tacit knowledge is stored in the Gorilla's corporate survival guide. That "Gorilla's Guide" serves as the script for your culture. To get a better look at the underlying dynamics of culture, let's take a brief detour to the Internet phenomenon called Wikipedia.

"Wikipedia" is derived from wiki, the Hawaiian word for fast. Wikipedia suggests a fast, comprehensive source of information. It is a free online encyclopedia written by anyone who wants to contribute, not just experts. Because it's online, hyperlinks in the articles allow you to access an article from many different places. For example, you might get to the article on "house" from hundreds of links embedded in numerous articles on topics such as civilization, Roman villa, McMansion, and cocoon.

What does Wikipedia have to do with corporate culture?

Imagine a Wikipedia where the information consists only of stories about events that have happened at your company. Now imagine that those stories are stored in employees' heads instead of the Internet. This Wikipedia of organizational life is your company's Gorilla's Guide. Every day, events at work are added to it. For example, consider this real incident at what became a well-known company. It demonstrates how the Gorilla's Guide works.

When the company's founding CEO arrived at work one morning, he happened upon a group of third-shift maintenance workers. He asked them to take a break to talk with him. After buying a round of orange juice for everyone, he asked the workers how the company could improve its customers' experiences. For about an hour, the CEO asked questions and listened as the maintenance workers shared their perspectives with him. After the impromptu meeting, the maintenance supervisor asked the CEO why he was meeting with the maintenance workers. The founder explained that he believed that good ideas can come from anyone, that creativity is everywhere.

Since it was a significant event for these maintenance workers to meet with the CEO, the story of this meeting hit the grapevine, circulated, and became part of the Gorilla's Guide. Over time, this company built a large entertainment empire based on its creativity and concern for its guests' experiences. That founding CEO was Walt Disney and this is a real story from the early days at Disneyland. Of course, this wasn't an isolated event; employees frequently heard many similar stories. The stories all became part of the company's Gorilla's Guide.

While consulting to a nonprofit organization that provided educational services for kids ages five through twelve, I got a sudden glimpse into one of the unspoken rules of the organization's culture. They had experienced several crises that caused parents to lose confidence in the school. The executive director was frustrated. She had been the associate executive director for years. She knew the history of these issues, and she knew she had to take action to turn things around. To begin rebuilding trust and confidence, we held an open meeting with parents. I had met with the board, which included several parent members, in advance to prepare for this meeting. While there was some divisiveness among the board and with the staff about the situation, they had come to some decisions about how to handle the issues. They had made commitments to each other about what they would say and how they would handle issues and questions at the upcoming parents' meeting. The board appeared to be ready to speak with one voice (as a board must). Yet, in the parents' meeting, those commitments and decisions repeatedly fell by the wayside as the conversation became more heated. I watched the executive director as her sense of impending doom built.

During a break, I talked privately with the executive director and her office manager. We discussed the way that many of the board members had seemingly forgotten the commitments they had made to speak with one voice. The office manager said simply, "Oh, that happens all the time around here. People tell you what they think you want to hear. Then they do whatever they want. It makes me crazy!"

No wonder the executive director was frustrated! Clearly, the Gorilla's Guide had plenty of stories of broken commitments and gaps between public statements and subsequent behavior. While this behavior was upsetting to some members of the organization, many people seemed to understand that it was simply "how things are done around here." The executive director and the board failed to manage the culture and the culture made it impossible to manage the other critical success factors.

Organizational culture is not an abstraction—it's personal. It is embodied in everyone in the company because you and all of your employees have these stories in your heads. Some of these are shared stories, perhaps circulated over the grapevine; others are specific to you, based on your personal experiences.

Let's go back to our Wikipedia analogy. When you access Wikipedia on your computer in New York City, you have access to exactly the same information I have in Austin, Texas. That's our shared Gorilla's Guide—everyone has a common set of stories. I also have information on the computer that I'm using to access Wikipedia that is different from what is on your computer, some of which is related to the Wikipedia information. The unique information we each have on our computer supplements our shared Wikipedia.

Similarly, while we have a shared Gorilla's Guide with common material, we also bring our unique experiences to our personal Gorilla's Guide. Some of the unique material is from events that happen in the organization that simply cannot be shared, for example, what your boss said in your one-on-one. Some is left over from other organizations you've worked for. Traces of the culture of those organizations influence you long after you have left the organization. (That's why hiring people who fit your culture is so important. More on that in Chapter 11, Second Nature the Behaviors.) What guides your behavior is the collection of shared stories, personalized by your unique experiences. The more time you spend in the organization, the more of the shared culture you absorb. In this way, it is both shared and personally unique.

This explains, for example, why the team in the Cincinnati field office doesn't operate the same way as the headquarters team in Chicago. Things happen in Cincinnati. These are added to the Cincinnati employees' Gorilla's Guide, not the Chicago Gorilla's Guide and vice versa. As one field rep told me, "They've got their way at headquarters, but out here in Cincinnati, our Gorilla doesn't play by the same rules."

The gap is even wider if the two locations are in different countries. At Wikipedia.org, you have a choice of different editions of Wikipedia in different languages. The content of each is different. The Italian Wikipedia doesn't have the same information as the English Wikipedia.

Your organization's culture is situated in the context of the national or ethnic culture. That makes the gap between the cultures at the Chicago headquarters and the Paris field office even wider than the gap between Chicago and Cincinnati.

The same thing often happens with different departments in the organization. The gap between marketing and engineering is partly due to the fact that each profession attracts different thinking styles. It's also a result of different Gorilla's Guides. We share maybe 80 percent of the Gorilla's Guide with the whole organization. But that 20 percent of content that is unique to marketing can cause problems when marketing is interacting with engineering.

The patterns in the Gorilla's Guide tell members of the organization what is expected of them. The web of stories forms an implicit set of directives about how to behave in the organization. Without even being aware that the culture is influencing them, employees are subtly nudged into alignment.

Many corporate alliances, including mergers, acquisitions, joint ventures, private equity deals, and others, fail to reach their potential because they can't reconcile the culture differences. The most challenging aspect of the integration or collaboration is creating enough of a shared culture quickly enough to enable work to get done. It's not a simple matter of setting new policies or developing a new organization chart. Creating a shared culture rarely shows up on the integration plan, but it is a complex and demanding task that is critical to success. That's one of the many situations in which managing culture is essential. This book is about managing culture with the same skills and commitment with which you manage other critical factors in your business.

CHAPTER 2

HOW YOUR CULTURE IS LIKE DISNEYLAND

The gorilla groups pass skills down from one generation to the next, from nest building to group leadership. Tiger was two and a half years old, past the age when most infants have begun to practice nest building. His first attempts were clumsy at best. "The youngster confidently began bending long stalks of foliage one by one onto his lap. Standing on all fours, he tried to push the springy stems beneath him, then hurriedly attempted to reseat himself on top of them. The uncooperative Senecio vegetation naturally sprang back into an upright position; his small body could not control all the stalks he had succeeded in breaking. Tiger repeated the process four times before his confidence gave vent to utter frustration" … It would be several months before he learned to build a sturdy nest. But eventually Tiger did master this important skill.

Gorillas in the Mist

New group members learn your culture just as Tiger's mother taught him to build a nest. The Gorilla's Guide is the medium through which your culture is passed on. If you want to manage your organization's culture, you first need to understand how the Gorilla's Guide works. Remember, organizational culture is not simply a concept—it's very real and personal. The Gorilla is embodied in everyone in the company, and it guides their decisions using the Gorilla's Guide. This helps reinforce "how things are done around here."

Three Principles

Understanding three basic principles of the Gorilla's Guide will help you see why culture can be hard to manage.

Employees Access the Gorilla's Guide without Even Thinking about It: Let's return to the story of the Disneyland maintenance workers. Having this story in the Gorilla's Guide affected how the employees paid attention to events at Disneyland. This story helped shape "how we do things around here," that is, the corporate culture. Disney built a culture of exceptional service.

Recently, Glen and his family took his cousin to Disneyland. Glen's cousin is autistic and at sixty-five years old, he had never been to Disneyland. Glen wanted his cousin to have a day he would always remember. When they arrived, they stopped at guest relations and explained the situation. The individual who assisted them made sure they got the royal treatment all day. They never had to wait in line. At each attraction, the host would ask, "Where are you going next?" When Glen told her, she would phone ahead to be sure the special treatment continued. Glen got misty-eyed telling me how much that day meant to his cousin and the entire family. It was an extraordinary experience because the Disneyland employees know that creating extraordinary moments is part of their job.

Employees Are Constantly Updating Their Gorilla's Guide: At Disneyland, many employees participated in creating the trip of a lifetime for Glen's cousin. Meanwhile, in other parts of the park, one person picked up a gum wrapper on her way to fix the broken ice cream machine. Another coworker stopped to help a family trying to find the nearest restroom. Other coworkers noticed all of these events, and they became part of both the individual and collective Gorilla's Guides in the organization. These updates are made as events unfold and without the employees' conscious attention.

This update process is behind the concept of emergent strategy. When you set a strategy, it drifts over time because of what is happening in the environment. This is why you can't truly manage products, customers, and finances without managing culture.

The Gorilla's Guide Shapes Behavior; Behavior Shapes the Gorilla's Guide: This is what leads to increasing consistency of behavior within a given culture, and it can get a bit confusing. It reminds me of *Drawing Hands* by M.C. Escher in which each hand is drawing the other.

Because employees, consciously or unconsciously, often model their behavior after their leaders, people in any given organization tend to behave in similar ways. This can also arise out of the nature of the environment, the purpose for which the organization exists, and hiring criteria. Because of these similarities in behavior, patterns begin to emerge in the stories in the Gorilla's Guide. These patterns form messages or directives that tell employees what matters to the organization and how to behave to meet the organization's expectations. This promotes ever more consistent behaviors, which creates a steady stream of new stories that support and reinforce organizational behavior. In this way, each company forms a distinctive culture, and the culture continually recreates itself. This self-reproducing quality is what makes culture so hard to change.

What does this mean for your strategy? Simply that if the stories in the Gorilla's Guide aren't consistent with the execution of your strategy, your culture will likely interfere with the strategy, regardless of how much time and energy you've invested in developing it. The Gorilla's Guide isn't printed in the employee handbook. It's stored in the hearts and minds of every member of the organization. Members of the organization do things "the way they've always been done," according to the patterns in the Gorilla's Guide. The only way to ensure your strategy will be executed is to be sure the culture supports the strategy. If you're not managing culture, you can't manage strategy.

Organizational culture determines whether the customer really comes first and quality really is "job #1." Or whether backstabbing and politics are really the best strategy instead. It decides whether your customer is treated as a transaction or as a person. By consciously creating your Gorilla's Guide, you can make your organization's culture into a strategic ally for performance. You can manage culture.

To Make a Profit or Not

Let's look at what happened in the mid-1990s at a computer company. For years, the company's management treated software mostly as a necessary part of the system, not something that created shareholder value. It's hard to imagine that now, but that approach was pretty common back then. About 10 percent of the company's employees worked in the software division, but the division's only customer was the company's hardware division. Software was seen as a cost item, not a revenue-generator.

By the mid-1990s, it became apparent all across the computer industry that software had huge potential to generate revenue growth. This computer systems company decided to turn its software division from a cost center to a profit center with external customers.

Hal was the newly appointed general manager of the software division. His top priority was making the shift from cost center to profit center. Hal and his executive team developed a comprehensive strategic plan, detailing the changes that would be made in financial models, product plans, sales strategies, and more. Executives and managers across the division were assigned goals with associated bonuses. Even so, Hal's strategy failed miserably. Things stayed pretty much as they had been before.

Why? The executives focused on managing the business model and product mix, not culture. The culture in the software division was dominated by a focus on cool technology. Because the division didn't have to go to the market for revenue and customers, the engineers ran the show. Regardless of the plans and budgets Hal and his team created, engineers worked on the projects they found exciting. Market focus was barely even a concept. The technical staff simply had no connection with the market. Their sense of power and importance in the company was derived entirely from elegant and leading edge technology projects. The Gorilla in this division was not interested in customers, markets, or revenue—only in "cool" technology.

This story is another example of how culture eats strategy for lunch. Of course, managers were given goals appropriate to the new business model. Sales and marketing created new teams, and they were staffed to support the new approach. Marketing carried out a software branding and marketing initiative. The employee communications group developed messages to convey the new strategy to everyone in the company. The Gorilla's Guide, however, was filled with stories about daily life in the organization, a life that revolved around "cool projects." When the official messages and systems are not in sync with the stories, the culture ignores the official systems.

The Gorilla's Guide: A Three-track Recording

The Gorilla's Guide is made up primarily of stories that carry messages. These stories and messages are recorded from three distinctly different sources, forming three tracks in the recording. Each track is laid down in a different way. Understanding how this recording works is the most critical item for you to master if you want to manage culture the way you manage products, customers, and finances. You wouldn't dream of hiring a CFO who couldn't read a balance sheet. For you to be adept at managing culture, this is the equivalent of learning to read a balance sheet. You will need to use different strategies and skills to influence the content of each track of the recording. Part Three is devoted to those strategies.

Track 1: Official Messages: This track consists of all the official, direct ways that organizations tell their employees what is expected of them. It includes a wide variety of things from the poster with your mission and values, to your strategy, to the criteria on your performance appraisal form. The nice thing about Track 1 is that you can control the content. It's important that this content be

- Clear and specific
- Consistent across all of the sources.

Some of these documents, for example, your mission statement and company values, may be somewhat abstract and general. Others should be very behaviorally specific, for example, your performance appraisal criteria or customer service policy. Both the general and the specific are important.

It's also essential that the messages about what you expect from employees are consistent across all of these communication tools. If "the customer comes first" is a part of your company values, then your problem escalation policies should be written to support fast resolution of customer problems, as much or more than to protect your senior support team from customers. If *experiment relentlessly* (Chapter 6) is a key message, that might be reflected in a practice of regularly conducting post-action learning debriefs.

If your ideals are reflected in the nuts and bolts of policies and processes in Track 1, you can work on getting stories into Track 2 that support the ideals. Those stories help the Gorilla get the message. That's why consistency in all the ways Track 1 is recorded really matters.

Track 2: Events: This track records actual events, either witnessed firsthand or gleaned from the grapevine. It's what employees see happening at work or hear on the grapevine about what has happened. You have much less control over Track 2 than over Track 1! You can influence this track primarily in two ways:

- Personal congruence
- Grapevine stories.

It's essential that your own actions be congruent with the official messages on Track 1. Otherwise, you aren't sending a clear signal about how you want members of the organization to behave. The Gorilla watches to see if what you say is congruent with what you do. If it's not, your behavior is more likely to be reflected in the culture than what you say.

You can also seed the grapevine with stories of others' successes, highlighting alignment with the official expectations for behavior. The more stories of aligned behavior that circulate on the grapevine, the faster your culture will shift.

As you read each directive in Part Two, ask yourself, "What events are occurring in my organization (and being recorded in Track 2) that either support or undermine this directive?" Do this mental exercise with clear-eyed realism. I'm not asking what you'd like to occur or have recorded; I'm asking you to think about what really occurs. That's what gets recorded in Track 2. In Part Three, we'll look at how you can influence these recordings.

Track 3: Interpretations: This track comes from the interpretations that people give to the events and stories on Track 2. When employees see something happen or hear about a decision, they make assumptions about why the events unfolded as they did. Mostly, these aren't even thought of as assumptions.

When we observe things, we think we "know" why they happened. That "knowledge" is usually a large leap of logic that is based on our prior experiences and our beliefs as much as it is based on what we observed. For example, when a peer is recognized for her contribution to a big account win and I am not, I "know" it's because she is located in the home office and I'm out of sight in a remote field location. In my organization, all of us "know" that corporate is clueless about what happens in the field. Most likely, I don't think of any of this as my assumptions; I think of it as facts. After all, we're all graduates of MSU (Making Stuff Up).

By providing explanations of your own decisions and actions, you can preempt some of these logic leaps. This gives you significant influence over Track 3.

Putting It All Together: Official messages, events, and interpretations— together all of these form the Gorilla's Guide. Stories are the essence of this three-track recording. Whether an event is witnessed firsthand or heard on the grapevine, the story is stored in the Gorilla's Guide. Not as a series of data points, but as a story. Our brains hold stories somewhat like a hologram. The sights, sounds, smells, and emotions are all captured along with the basic events. We remember stories longer and more vividly than we remember facts. The power and durability of the culture are a result of these rich stories.

Understanding how these three different kinds of information become part of your culture gives you the knowledge to consciously contribute to all three tracks of the recording. This allows you to manage culture effectively.

Johnson & Johnson's Gorilla's Guide

In 1943, General Robert Wood Johnson wrote the first Johnson & Johnson Credo which encapsulates the organization's ideal Gorilla's Guide. It begins, "We believe our first responsibility is to the doctors, nurses, and patients, to mothers and fathers and all others who use our products and services." This is an important part of Track 1 (official messages) at Johnson & Johnson.

Those words on the page were constantly reinforced. Thirty years after the credo was written, in the mid-1970s, the Johnson & Johnson chairman started a process of credo challenge sessions that helped keep the credo in sync with the times and helped managers stay aligned with the credo. Over the years, the credo was embodied in performance management systems, meeting agendas, promotion policies, and many other policies and procedures. Many incidents helped fill the Gorilla's Guide with stories showing the credo in action.

Then, in 1982, the Tylenol tampering incident occurred, in which several people died as a result of poisoned Tylenol capsules. Johnson & Johnson executive management chose to get the product off the shelves immediately everywhere in the United States. The cost of the recall was estimated at $75 million. The Johnson & Johnson credo was so embedded in the culture that this was the obvious choice—the link to the credo wasn't even discussed explicitly until after the decision had been made. Consider how different this story is from other similar incidents such as the Ford/Firestone episode and Merck's problems with Vioxx.

The bottom-line result? The immediate impact was a significant loss in market share and a 10 percent drop in Johnson & Johnson's stock price. But, within about five months, Tylenol had regained 70 percent of its former market share and within three years, it had returned to its pre-crisis market share. Brand loyalty was strengthened, and Johnson & Johnson emerged as a clear winner. Of course, the whole incident got stored in the Gorilla's Guide. The events in Track 2 and the interpretations in Track 3 were well-aligned with the Track 1 messages in the credo.

The Johnson & Johnson story helps us see how culture affects your organization's success. Employees make hundreds of decisions every day. A customer service representative decides what attitude to convey to the customer when he calls. A manufacturing supervisor decides what to do about a small imperfection. A sales representative decides whether to make one more call before she goes home. Each one of those decisions makes a difference to the organization's bottom line and each is influenced by your culture. You can't directly control each decision, but you can manage the culture.

Trust

The Johnson & Johnson story also illustrates the importance of trust. Following the Tylenol incident, Johnson & Johnson worked hard to regain its customers' trust. Trust is a critical foundation for your success. Without it, the fabric of your organization will always be weak. You can temporarily motivate people with fear, but fear will block the connections, creativity, and collaboration that you need for sustained success.

In Part Two, we'll cover six directives that are essential to making your culture a competitive advantage. Trust isn't one of them. That's because trust really can't be pulled out as a separate item. Each of the directives includes behaviors that exemplify trust and none of the directives can be fulfilled without trust. Trust must be part of everything you do.

When we pull out trust as a separate issue, it's too easy to let it become an abstraction. Trust as an abstraction doesn't improve your organization. Trusting behaviors do. Your Gorilla's Guide needs to be filled with stories that support trust.

Mike was the general manager of the Intercontinental Division at Tandem. I joined his organization in 1990. Like many people, my corporate career had left me with some bumps and bruises from managers who were less than wonderful. I didn't have much reason to trust "management" but I trusted Mike. He had a reputation for treating people fairly and at the same time getting business results. He trusted his managers to do the right thing and they generally didn't disappoint him. With a geographic responsibility that spread from Canada to Asia and Australia, Mike couldn't possibly control everything, but the mutual trust on his team made it work.

Don't let trust be just an abstraction in your organization. Make it part of the very fiber of your being. Before you hire someone, be sure his behaviors will support the high standards you set for trust. It's the foundation of everything you do.

Looking at Strategy through the Gorilla's Eyes

Now that you have a better understanding of how culture works, you'll want to review your business strategy. You've probably thought about the big issues, for example, new skills or technologies as part of your strategic planning. Culture operates at a more subtle level, reflecting and shaping day-to-day behavior. One of the biggest risks associated with your strategy is whether the culture will support it. Identify the elements of the strategy that will need to be supported by the culture, then manage the culture as proactively as you manage the rest of the strategy.

As you review the strategy, consider what small decisions and behaviors might need to be in place for the strategy to be successful. What will employees need to see as important? Where will they need to focus their attention?

To a large extent, your culture regulates these things based on what is in the Gorilla's Guide. If your strategy calls for customer relationships that are both broad and deep, is that part of your current culture? Does your culture value those relationships, or is it focused primarily on efficient transactions? Of course, some of that gap can be closed with knowledge, skills, processes, and other elements of the official systems. But now that you've seen how the three-track recording of the Gorilla's Guide works, you know that's not enough.

PART TWO

THE DIRECTIVES

A crucial step in creating a culture that is a competitive advantage for your organization is identifying the directives and behaviors that will drive that culture. The next six chapters will help you do that. Each chapter focuses on one directive:

- *Question rigorously*
- *Include respectfully*
- *Commit responsibly*
- *Experiment relentlessly*
- *Integrate radically*
- *Connect, really*

A brief explanation of the term "directives" may be helpful here. Each directive is written as an imperative statement to underscore the idea that the Gorilla's Guide is telling members of your organization what to do. Directives are similar to values in that they address how people act on a day-to-day basis. You may decide to adopt these six directives as your organizational values. Or you may decide to create a more personal or philosophical statement to support the directives and serve as your organizational values. In that case, these directives will serve as a bridge between values and action.

For each directive, you'll learn behaviors that will make the directive real, beliefs that may hinder your success, actions you can take to support the directive, and multicultural opportunities and challenges associated with that directive.

These directives, actions, and challenges are relevant to you whether you are a senior executive in a large organization, a leader somewhere else in the organization, or a small business owner. Whatever your position in the organization, you can be a leader.

Some challenges are specific to the team at the top. The CEO and his direct reports (the C-level team) have a unique role in the organization that offers both opportunities and challenges in managing the culture of an organization. As you read each directive, watch for the *C-level teams* section, where I'll address those concerns.

It's essential that you actively engage with this material. Look at each directive to see how you would adapt the key behaviors to fit your circumstances. Think about how the directive would support your strategy. Make notes in the book about how you would use the directive. Talk to your staff about how to apply the behaviors in your organization. Make it truly yours. Begin managing your culture now.

CHAPTER 3

QUESTION RIGOROUSLY

What could alarm a large, silverback male gorilla? Poachers? Another gorilla group encroaching on his territory? One sunny afternoon on the western slopes of the mountain, Fossey heard cries of alarm from Uncle Bert, the silverback. She assumed something dreadful must be happening as she approached the group. Suddenly she saw a pair of ravens dive-bombing Uncle Bert as he cringed, covering his head with his hands and screaming out his alarm. Fossey's unquestioned assumptions flew off with the ravens.

Gorillas in the Mist

Like Fossey, your team may have some assumptions that just don't match reality. When you are working on a problem or making a decision, it's important to know what you know and what you don't know. That's only possible if your culture values questions as much as answers and distinguishes between assumptions and facts. If it does, it will be much easier to make good decisions, even when you don't know all the answers to your questions. On the other hand, if this directive to *question rigorously* isn't part of your Gorilla's Guide, you can end up with meetings that take too long, decisions that aren't sound, and unpleasant surprises.

Here's what happened with the executive team of a regional restaurant group. Marika took over as CEO about a year ago. Since the board had removed the previous CEO, it was a difficult transition. Marika had replaced two top-level executives, promoting one person inside the organization and bringing in one new executive from the outside. The team was beginning to gel. However, Marika complained that they spent too much time talking and too little time doing. After a particularly long discussion during one executive staff meeting, the team reached a difficult strategy decision. After the meeting, Marika was exasperated. "That decision should have taken us less than an hour; it took us over two hours."

You've probably been in meetings like that. By using the behaviors in this chapter, Marika sharpened the team's ability to distinguish between facts and assumptions. She persuaded their Gorilla to *question rigorously*. This significantly improved the team's use of meaningful information to make decisions. Marika was relieved to see that the quality of their decisions improved, their confidence in their decisions grew, and their meetings got shorter.

Going to Abilene

On the other hand, there is the well-known trip to Abilene. In case you're not familiar with the Abilene Paradox, here's the basic idea. Two couples end up driving fifty-three miles to Abilene, Texas, for dinner on a hot July night (104 degrees!) in a car without any air-conditioning. The paradox? None of them actually wanted to go, but they each made assumptions about what the others thought and felt. If you've ever been to West Texas in the summer, you can imagine their feelings.

Jerry Harvey, author of *The Abilene Paradox*, summed it up this way. "Here we were, four reasonably sensible people who—of our own volition—had just taken a 106-mile trip across a godforsaken desert in a furnace-like heat and a dust storm to eat unpalatable food at a hole-in-the-wall cafeteria in Abilene, when none of us had really wanted to go."

Most people have been on a work team that took a trip to Abilene at some point. Remember that decision your team made and everyone later said they didn't want it but just went along with the team? Occasionally, those afterthoughts may be a simple case of people trying to distance themselves from a bad decision. However, it is often a sign that your team is allowing assumptions to go unchallenged. If your Gorilla embraces the directive to *question rigorously*, your team will value questions as much as answers, sort facts from assumptions and opinions, and thoroughly explore differences of opinion.

What's the big deal if you don't? The trip to Abilene doesn't take that long. And it doesn't happen that often, right? But if you care about execution speed, it is a big deal. There are three ways that unchallenged assumptions (and the occasional trip to Abilene) block effective execution.

Resources are wasted: Obviously, when you take that unnecessary trip to Abilene, you're wasting gas. Resources that could have been invested in your strategy are being wasted on something that the team didn't need to do. Given the pressure most organizations are under to do more with less, you can't afford that waste of resources.

Decisions don't stick: If discussions don't provide a way to expose and challenge assumptions, there's a good chance that decisions won't stick. When assumptions aren't surfaced, it often turns out that each team member had a different understanding of the situation or the decision. As execution gets underway, team members will likely feel a need to revisit the decision as the different interpretations become clear. You know what that means—more meetings! Instead of getting something done, you'll find yourself having another meeting on that same decision. What a waste of time!

People aren't accountable: Unspoken assumptions interfere with accountability. Accountability is crucial to execution, and the #1 enemy of accountability is unasked questions and unchallenged assumptions. When someone commits to a goal and no one asks questions about how the goal will be achieved, two things happen. First, the individual making the commitment gets off easy. He doesn't have to provide his peers with answers to the hard questions. Second, other members of the team may have inadequate insight to determine if the goal is at risk. How can you hold each other accountable if you lack the information to understand the issues and challenges affecting the goal?

If team members don't get a chance to fully explore the issues by asking questions, challenging assumptions, expressing disagreements, and so forth, it's way too easy for them to duck responsibility later. You've heard those comments. "No one really understood Joe's plan anyway," or "I knew this wouldn't work." These are sure signs that too much was left unsaid.

Wasted resources, decisions that don't stick, and lack of accountability—all of these undermine your efforts to manage your organization's critical success factors. By managing your culture, you can prevent those things from happening.

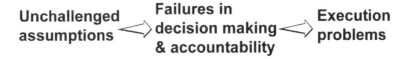

Execution suffers when assumptions go unchallenged and questions go unasked. You can prevent those problems if your Gorilla has a directive to *question rigorously*. This doesn't mean you have to wait until you have all the facts to make a decision. That would often be disastrous. In fact, you'll find you can make decisions more quickly when you learn to *question rigorously*.

Why We Prefer Abilene

We don't *question rigorously* because we want to avoid three things.

Vulnerability: Many people feel that asking questions is a sign of weakness because you're admitting you don't know everything. The feeling of vulnerability associated with admitting you don't have all the answers may block you from asking questions. Of course, heading down the wrong path because you didn't ask the hard questions or challenge assumptions leaves you pretty vulnerable, too! Using questions effectively signals your team that it's okay not to have all the answers.

Action items: Sometimes, a team member would like to raise a question, but he's pretty sure that no one on the team has the answer. That means that if it's an important question, he is likely to be tasked with finding the answer. Great—another action item. Bet that's just what he wanted! But the question needs to be raised anyway. As your team discusses issues, don't assume the person who raised the question will resolve it. Consider who is the logical owner for this new action item.

Conflicts: Perhaps the most problematic reason that we don't raise questions and concerns is that we don't want to deal with the conflict that may arise. It's as if somewhere in the back of our minds, a little voice says, "Let's see ... conflict or Abilene? I'll take Abilene." For your Gorilla to really live the directive to *question rigorously*, you must be willing to engage in constructive conflict.

I Don't Know

With all those barriers to your team's ability to *question rigorously*, what can you do to manage your culture? The first action you can take as a leader is very simple. Say, "I don't know" simply and directly. Set an example of not knowing so others realize it's okay not to have all the answers. Ask for help or input whenever it is useful.

When Kai was promoted to Eastern region vice president, she got off to a rocky start. She had come up through the ranks and still operated more like an area director than a vice president. Employees saw her as a know-it-all. Frequently Kai posed a problem for her team. Then when they came up with a solution, she would tell them the solution she had already decided on. The team was about ready to revolt.

Kai and I talked about the lack of trust in her team and its roots in her desire to avoid feeling vulnerable. She wanted her team to see her as adding value and she believed that having all the answers would make that happen. Kai first began experimenting with sharing her vulnerability in very small ways, then over time in more significant ways. She disciplined herself to acknowledge when she didn't have the answer. Months later, one of the directors in Kai's organization told me that the single biggest change since Kai and I had started working on her leadership was that "Kai admits she doesn't have all the answers." He felt that as a result of that, the team had developed a level of trust and candor they had never had and was well on its way to its best year ever.

```
Key Behavior:
Say "I don't know."
```

Saying "I don't know" models the idea that not knowing is a legitimate part of problem-solving. It also builds trust, makes assumptions visible, and prevents unpleasant surprises.

Watch Your Head

The foundation of *question rigorously* is your ability to observe and improve your own thinking. Whenever I see "watch your head" on a low doorframe, I laugh. Of course, I can't literally watch my head! The practices I'm going to discuss in this section have a bit of that same dilemma. I'm going to ask you to observe your own thinking, that is, watch what goes on inside your head. Because you're the one doing the thinking, this is a bit tricky at first. With these tools and disciplined attention on your part, you'll be able to do it, and you'll be amazed at how it improves your thinking. See-ing your thinking is essential to learning to *question rigorously*. After all, if you can't see something, it's pretty hard to improve it.

One way to see your thinking more clearly is to use what Lauren Pow-ers called the Rat Brain Loop in *The Trouble with Thinking*. Powers says our thinking has four parts:

1 Select information to pay attention to from the billions of bits of data we are exposed to.

2 Decide what that data means.

3 Attach labels (often unflattering ones) to ourselves or others based on that meaning.
4 React based on those labels.

This whole process takes place outside of our awareness. Yikes—my reaction that seemed so justified and rational was based on this emotionally charged, unaware thinking? Powers says yes.

The cure for this messy state of affairs is to reflect on the four parts of your thinking and then share that with the other person who was involved in the event or conversation. You can use the four parts of your thinking to help expose assumptions and clarify where things went wrong.[1] This process is a great tool to make your reflection time more powerful.

Focused Reflection

The most underutilized resource that most organizations have for executive development is reflection. It doesn't cost a thing, and you can improve your problem-solving, decision-making and communication skills dramatically by investing as little as fifteen minutes a day in focused reflec-tion. I realize that fifteen minutes of quiet thinking time may seem like a rare luxury, but the payoff is huge. The time you spend unraveling problems will decrease dramatically, thus giving you back far more than you've invested. This is more than a review of your day, although that is a reason-able starting point. It's an opportunity to use the tools discussed in this chapter to change the way you think. Focused reflection gives you the abil-ity to change your thinking in ways that make a real difference to your results. Consider it a software upgrade for your personal operating system.

An easy way to begin using reflection for your own development is to schedule fifteen minutes for a quiet review of your day. Sit down with a pen

---

[1] For a great tool from Power's book, go to www.FourthFactorOnline.com under Resources.

and paper (or your PDA) and review a few activities or events in your day to see where you were effective and where you'd like to improve. Write some notes to yourself. Next, begin adding some probing questions to your reflection. The idea is to lead yourself into uncomfortable areas that help you become more aware of your own thinking processes and assumptions.

For example, try this exercise. Think about a recent event or meeting. Review your own behavior and statements as if you are watching a video recording in your mind. As you watch, make up an interpretation of your actions that is very different from what you intended. You might do this by imagining what an adversary or someone who is critical of you might think. Looking through that lens, find data to justify the erroneous interpretation you invented. Or, you can look at the meanings you have assigned to someone else's actions and search creatively for data that contradicts your meaning. Doing this will help you see how data is filtered and meanings are assigned. You'll start to really experience the fact that any event or action can be interpreted in many ways. This will help you see your own assumptions and improve your thinking. You become both a participant and an observer. If this process isn't uncomfortable sometimes, producing thoughts that surprise you, then you're not going deep enough. Keep probing.

Key Behavior:
Practice merciless self-awareness; reflect often and uncomfortably.

One practical note about using focused reflection. Many executives use their commute home to review their day. That's a start, but it isn't an ideal setting for the aspects of reflection that require you to dig deeper. You need to focus all of your attention on the reflection. Most people find that it helps to write down some thoughts. If you drive or walk to work, that's not the best setting for your reflection—your attention is divided between getting where you are going safely and your reflection. And you can't write while you drive or walk. If you commute by train or bus and can find a quiet spot to sit, that may work. In general, you'll get more value from your reflection time if you close your office door and dedicate fifteen minutes to your own development through reflection.

Keeping Your Team out of Abilene

Seeing and challenging assumptions in your team is a crucial part of strategic planning. Scenario planning is a strategy development tool that is useful in learning to see multiple possible futures. In *The Living Company*, Arie de Geus wrote that we don't see the impending failure of our plans because we see only what we expect to see. We see what we are looking for, not necessarily what we are looking at. Learning to see multiple possible futures can be very helpful in removing some of the organizational blocks and unseen assumptions that leave us open to being blindsided by events. Because our assumptions often cause us to see only one possible future, we may miss clues that tell us what is really unfolding. Individually, you can use focused reflection to expose your own assumptions and improve the quality of your insights. As a team, you can use scenario planning the same way.

We'll discuss three other techniques you can use with your team.

Left-hand Column: Chris Argyris called this the left-hand column exercise. The idea is that while we are participating in a discussion, a second conversation is often occurring in our heads. Sometimes we are aware of those thoughts, and we don't feel we can share them with others. Other times, the thoughts sort of skitter past, just out of our awareness.

Here is a short summary of what Argyris recommended. Think back to a recent conversation that was emotionally charged or somehow difficult for you, preferably one that occurred in the last day or two. Divide a sheet of paper into two columns. In the right column, record the conversation as you remember it. In the left column opposite each right column statement, record what you thought or felt but didn't say. (See Senge's *The Fifth Discipline Fieldbook: Strategies and Tools for Building a Learning Organization* for more detail.)

What you thought but didn't say	What was said

You'll find this process much easier and more rewarding if you've already had some experience with the probing reflection we discussed previously. Otherwise, it may not turn up anything new or surprising.

Doing this exercise with your team can help you see your assumptions. When one executive team tried this technique after a heated discussion, their left columns had thoughts like: "There's no point in arguing.

George has made up his mind." "Here we go again, playing 'blame the services guy.'"

Each of those left column statements has assumptions embedded in it. While you may not want to express your left column thoughts exactly as they occur to you, becoming more conscious of these thoughts allows you to see your assumptions. If you feel the team is playing "blame the services guy," that may suggest that you feel services is being scapegoated. Perhaps you see a larger systems dynamic that others are ignoring. Even if you don't know what that dynamic is, you can use your awareness of your left-hand column to raise the issue for discussion.

Key Behavior:
Expose your thinking.

While raising the issue may be uncomfortable, it builds trust in your team. You create an opportunity for a more open discussion. In the previous example, several of your colleagues may also see this discussion as an attempt to lay blame on the services group instead of solving the problem. By raising the question, you lead your team in developing more trust.

Uncovering the Pictures: It's not always easy to see when assumptions are being made in team discussions. If you sense that agreement is being reached too easily, the team might be basing its decision on untested assumptions. Each team member might have a different picture in mind. When those pictures don't match and aren't shared, circular discussions or delays in execution can result. Ask someone to make her picture specific and explicit for the group. Ask questions until you are very clear about what the person is thinking. Be sure other team members are also asking questions, not attacking or supporting the speaker's ideas. Then ask if anyone else has a different picture. This process gently exposes disconnects. In the discussion that follows, you have a much better opportunity to *question rigorously* because you've just gotten a lot of information, and maybe some assumptions, on the table.

Another strategy for making your assumptions visible is to attempt to intentionally violate your assumptions. Do something that seems completely counterintuitive. Propose a solution that is something "we don't do around here." I'm not suggesting you do something unethical, simply something that is different from your usual pattern. It's easiest to see our beliefs and assumptions when they are violated.

Balancing Asking and Telling: Most organizational cultures tend to value answers more than questions. Conversations tend to be dominated by telling, not leaving much room for asking. When the pace picks up, there is even less space for asking, and people get defensive. In that situation, it's very hard to *question rigorously* and ask the hard questions. How can you turn the situation around?

For the answer to this question, let's turn to Mr. Morgan, my ninth-grade science teacher. On a hot day right before school was out for the summer, Mr. Morgan was just as ready for summer break as we were, but there were a few more things he had to get through to us before we left for the summer. On this particular day, he picked up a ball from his desk, looked around at us, tossed the ball up, and caught it.

"What just happened?" he asked.

"The ball went up and came back down," a student replied, confident, but puzzled over the strangely simple question.

Mr. Morgan shook his head, tossed the ball, caught it, and asked, "What just happened?"

Another student replied, "You tossed the ball up, it came down, and you caught it."

Again, Mr. Morgan shook his head, tossed the ball, caught it, and again asked, "What just happened?"

A third student ventured, "The ball went up, it turned around, and it came down."

"Close enough," replied Mr. Morgan, smiling. "The ball went up, it stopped, then it came down."

Mr. Morgan wanted us to see that before the ball could change directions, it had to stop.

That's exactly what must happen before you can shift the conversation in a meeting from rapid-fire telling to open-ended asking. First, notice if the pace is speeding up. If the pace of the conversation seems fast to you, push the pause button. You might say, "Hang on a minute. This is too rapid-fire for us to consider the ideas." Then pause—create a silent space. This is when the ball stops before it begins its descent. Then, begin to ask questions, shifting the conversation toward a better balance of asking and telling.

What do you ask after the pause? Here are a few examples:

- How did you reach that conclusion?
- What would happen if we didn't do that?
- How would it affect our customers if we moved more quickly?
- What would it mean to our plans if that weren't true?

These and other open-ended questions will help you identify assumptions and make better decisions. Notice that none of the questions on this list begins with "why." When you start a question with "why," it tends to feel like an interrogation. The listener feels he must defend himself, even if you didn't intend it as an attack. Formulate some of your own questions that explore the underlying logic of a position or concept without asking "why."

**Key Behavior:
Balance telling and asking.**

Attack Problems, Not People

A key principle in *question rigorously* is to attack problems, not people. That phrase has been somewhat overused in recent years. The most basic level of application of the principle is ensuring that your discussion is focused on the ideas and issues rather than personalities. That means you'll hear comments like, "I don't agree with what Anil said. The market research my group has done indicates …" You won't hear, "Anil doesn't know what he's talking about." Applying the principle of attacking problems, not people, in this basic way will prevent the interpersonal sniping that derails trust.

Apply the principle more proactively to create a supportive, trusting environment in which team members can safely question and challenge each other. To do that, make it a habit to acknowledge others' contributions before you disagree or challenge them. Find something of value in what has been said and acknowledge it. For example, "Anil's customer anecdotes give us a useful view. For a different view, I'd like to share the market research data that my team has assembled." This takes the discussion from adversarial to collaborative. This example also illustrates how we can respect many different ways of knowing. (See Chapter 4, *Include Respectfully*, for more on this.) A collaborative, inclusive approach to discussions is essential for building the trust that supports your team in challenging assumptions.

**Key Behavior:
Attack issues, not people.**

In a collaborative discussion, it's much easier to engage effectively with questions, challenges, and disagreements. If you don't see value in the content that was presented, you can acknowledge the speaker for offering a different viewpoint. The idea is to create conversations where the exchange is open and collaborative so disagreements are more frequent and more productive.

Trouble Signs

How can you tell if your team doesn't *question rigorously* in a productive way? There are three signs to watch for. Any of these may happen occasionally, even in an organization that is adept at challenging assumptions. If they happen frequently, you're in danger.

Surprises: The executive team at a small healthcare company recently decided to restructure the reporting relationships between its healthcare facilities and the corporate organization to provide more focus and accountability. In one region, the changes were implemented on time with little confusion. In the other region, the changes stalled. What happened?

When the decision was made, Kaplan, the regional director in the second region, had serious concerns about the plan. However, when the team discussed the issue, Kaplan didn't voice his concerns. To make matters worse, his colleagues didn't ask him the "how" questions when he committed to the implementation plan. They all assumed Kaplan was on the same page they were. This sort of surprise is the first sign that your team needs to improve its ability to *question rigorously*.

Unresolved Conflicts: Another fairly common scenario is the shouting match in the conference room. The loudest voice wins instead of the most logical position. As a result, many issues aren't aired, and much that is said isn't heard or considered. In one executive team meeting in a large financial services company, a difficult decision had to be made. At first, the conflict was constructive. The discussion was on the right path. Then it became heated. The same people were saying the same things—only louder and faster. No one was really considering the ideas anymore. Team members stopped presenting new data and opinions, and the conversation became circular and repetitive.

Luis, the senior executive, became increasingly frustrated. He could have used his growing frustration as a signal to help the team see its pattern. Instead, Luis pounded his fist on the table and said (loudly), "I'm tired of this argument. Here is the solution we'll implement."

If this is a common scenario in your team, you likely aren't challenging assumptions and asking questions when you need to be. Your conflicts aren't productive. Your decisions may be faulty, and your team may fail to buy in to the decisions. Execution suffers.

We've talked about your left-hand column. When a discussion isn't going well, you may find your left-hand column overflowing. You have your own beliefs and ideas about what is being said, but you don't think you can raise these ideas in the conversation. Maybe it's already too loud and fast. Maybe a power dynamic is at play that makes silence seem like the prudent choice. In either case, as your left-hand column fills to overflowing, your frustration rises. That's a sure sign that assumptions, including your own, aren't being exposed and challenged.

Trips to Abilene: The executive team of a Dallas-based service company with just over150 employees decided it was time to create a free-standing product to complement its service offerings. The development and launch went well. Early user feedback was positive. The executive team felt that if only the product team had more resources, the product would have more features, and amazing growth would be possible. Their solution was to shut down one of the three existing service lines and hire people for the product team. This service line was the oldest and least exciting part of the business. The revenue and profits from this line weren't that big and growth was unlikely. The company phased out the service line. Six months later, revenue went down across all service lines. It soon became clear that this service was a key entry point for customers. No one had asked the hard questions about connections between this service and others. No one had challenged the assumption that revenue and growth potential were the most important criteria for keeping a particular service line. The decision proved disastrous; the company was unable to recover.

Not all bad decisions are trips to Abilene. Sometimes, a team does a great job of challenging assumptions and simply places the wrong bet. But if you look back on the decision making process and find too many unasked questions, then you've probably just gone to Abilene. That's a sign that your Gorilla doesn't *question rigorously* well. It's a sign that you are risking your ability to manage other critical success factors by not managing culture.

Multicultural Teams[2]

Question rigorously is all about how we think. One challenge in getting your culture to embrace this directive is the different ways all of us relate to change and uncertainty. While each of us has challenges in this area, it may be helpful to consider some cultural patterns. In many cultures, there is substantial avoidance of change. For example, Asian cultures place a high value on traditions. Challenging assumptions or asking hard questions may be seen as lacking proper respect for tradition. European cultures may place more emphasis on rules and regulations, making it difficult to consider overturning assumptions and beliefs that align with the rules. An awareness of these differences and an open dialog about the need for challenging assumptions and asking questions will help your team take a more inclusive approach to learning to *question rigorously*.

---

[2] It would take much more space than I have here to thoroughly explore the nuances of different cultures. These broad generalizations in this and subsequent chapters are provided simply to encourage you to see the many different ways people in different cultures may experience the messages in your Gorilla's Guide. For more details, see the *Cultural Communication Guide* by Cook Ross, Inc., or other similar resources focused on multicultural issues.

Differences in communication styles within multicultural teams can also pose a challenge. One aspect that is particularly relevant to *question rigorously* is the use of silence. In Native American cultures, several moments of silence is expected between speakers to make a space for everyone to consider what was said. In Arab and Asian cultures, silence for contemplation is also a typical part of the rhythm of conversation. In the Anglo American culture however, conversation is often rapid fire, with little or no room to consider one speaker's ideas before the next speaker begins. European cultures are somewhere between the two, with a polite formality that produces a more measured pace of discussion.

Consider the challenge of having all of these different rhythms in one conversation. Different members of the group will be frustrated for different reasons. Some people will speak more than others. Assumptions may be made about the interest or competence of group members. What a mess! The technique we discussed in the section on balancing telling and asking can be helpful in creating a rhythm of conversation that allows everyone to participate more fully.

Question rigorously often creates constructive conflict. Different cultural orientations toward conflict require multicultural awareness. More traditional cultures, for example, Latino, Arab, African, and Asian, place more emphasis on respect for authority and conformity while Western European and Anglo American cultures tend to favor open disagreement and dealing directly with differences of opinion. Still, within Western European and Anglo American cultures, many people avoid conflict to preserve harmony.

The last set of misunderstandings that often arise as teams *question rigorously* is gender differences in communication styles. Men and women tend to have different approaches to questioning. For example, if a woman has a fact or opinion, she may choose to raise her issue in the form of a question. On the other hand, even when a man doesn't have facts, he may express his view as a definitive statement. For men and women, questions may be heard as a sign of weakness or lack of knowledge; statements can sound like arrogance.

I once worked with an all-male executive team in a young technology company to improve their decision-making. They were unable to make good decisions because they talked on top of each other. Team members rarely explored what was behind a colleague's opinion before arguing with him. As they were discussing an important point in their strategy, I asked them to pause the discussion and then continue with one change—half the team was assigned the task of only asking questions. At first, those team members were silent. They couldn't think of any questions about this crucial topic.

After a few moments, Mark ventured in with a statement disguised as a question—"I think Oleg is overestimating the size of the market, don't you?" It took some trial and error before they were able to ask genuinely exploratory questions.

The point is simply that male culture tends to be statement-oriented, and female culture tends to be more question-oriented. A blend of the two approaches can be fruitful, even though there may be misunderstandings along the way. As with most differences in communication style, the best solutions are produced when all team members can value and engage the best of one another's thoughts.

The Bottom Line

The directive to *question rigorously* involves difficult and messy work. It's not the assumptions that we are conscious of that get us in trouble—it's the ones that we don't know we have. They are so ingrained in our culture or personal history that we consider them to be how the world works, not assumptions or beliefs. The ability to reflect and talk in sufficient depth and openness to allow the disruption of our basic assumptions is an important part of managing culture. Learning to *question rigorously* is a vital and central leadership task.

If you do this messy work, what do you get?

Decisions That Stick: Because members of your team have an opportunity to fully explore the issues, they are less likely to feel a need to revisit decisions that have already been made. Of course, the situation sometimes changes, and you need to revisit a decision. But the times when you have to have the whole discussion again because a team member didn't understand the issues or didn't feel heard should diminish radically.

Shorter Meetings: The time spent in circular conversations will diminish along with the time spent arguing at cross purposes. Instead, most of your time will be spent exploring the facts, asking hard questions, and having important and productive disagreements.

Fewer Trips to Abilene: Because you are making a space for genuine exploration of ideas and opinions, the chance that you'll end up someplace no one wanted to go drops significantly.

Action Plan:
Question Rigorously

- Say "I don't know."
- Practice merciless self-awareness; reflect often and uncomfortably.
- Expose your thinking.
- Balance telling and asking
- Attack issues, not people.

CHAPTER 4

INCLUDE RESPECTFULLY

Macho, an adult female in Uncle Bert's group, was often harassed by the other females in the group. Fossey describes her as walking "as though treading on eggshells" whenever she approached the other females. Macho soon became the group's scapegoat and was increasingly introverted. Eventually she developed a nervous tic. She remained a member of Uncle Bert's group, but was forced to remain on the fringes.

Gorillas in the Mist

If you've ever been in Macho's position in a workgroup, you probably still remember how it felt and how much your contribution to the group declined as you were increasingly marginalized. You don't want even subtle exclusionary behaviors in your organization. Your culture must be truly inclusive to reap the benefits of a diverse workforce. Inclusion is no longer optional. It isn't something you delegate to human resources or do only to be politically correct. There are many reasons why inclusion is critical to your success. I want to focus on two: the market and innovation.

What is the face of your market? Is it uniform and homogenous, or is it diverse and heterogeneous? Most likely, it's diverse, a mix of people from different ethnic groups, nationalities, genders, religions, and sexual orientations. It's people with different thinking styles, worldviews, abilities, and disabilities. Will a diverse team understand that market, anticipate its needs, and intuit its preferences better than a homogenous team? Pretty likely. But so far, we're only talking about diversity. To create a high performing diverse team, your Gorilla must also master inclusion.

One nonprofit CEO, lamenting the lack of diversity on his board, put it this way. "Our client population is very diverse. Ethnicity, socioeconomic background, abilities and disabilities, family status, age—you name it. How do we expect a bunch of middle-class, middle-aged white guys to understand and anticipate their concerns?"

Good question! Dealing with this issue doesn't mean that your organization's demographics have to mirror those of your target market perfectly. But it does mean that your culture must support both diversity and inclusion.

You know that innovation is vital to your success. Innovation and change are more easily fostered when there are differences. Let's take a simple example. Given a puzzle to solve, mixed gender teams will often outperform teams of all women or all men. Why? Men and women tend to have different patterns of thinking and communicating. The mixed gender teams thus have a broader set of mental resources available to them. In systems language, this is part of the "law of requisite variety." According to this law, the system with more variety will prevail over the one with less variety.

At the end of each of the other directives, we discuss several challenges and opportunities in a multicultural workforce. In each of those discussions, you see differences in ways of thinking, assumptions, and worldviews. When those differences come together in a respectful, open way, the team brain has access to enormous resources. Differences, creatively engaged, foster innovation. Building a culture of inclusion is how you make that happen.

Include respectfully is not about giving members of historically disadvantaged groups a chance or any other socially-conscious motivation. Being socially conscious is a good thing, but the business driver for inclusion is your organization's success.

Diversity Isn't Enough

Let's distinguish between two important terms: diversity and inclusion. These two words are sometimes used interchangeably, but when we are discussing culture, we need to clarify the distinction. As we will use it here, diversity means having a heterogeneous workforce. This may include differences in ethnicity, gender, religion, sexual orientation, abilities, disabilities, and other visible or invisible differences. We will use inclusion to refer not to who is in the workforce but to how people treat each other, what the Gorilla expects of members of both dominant and non-dominant groups in the workplace. Diversity and inclusion, as we are using these terms, are related ideas, but they are not the same.

Lack of diversity, the "middle-aged white guys" issue lamented by the CEO above, is a problem in terms of your connection and responsiveness to your market. Look at your executive team, your board of directors, your sales force, and your entire company. Do those groups look at least somewhat like your market? If not, your organization lacks the diversity that is essential to your success.

If your culture is not inclusive, that's a problem too. It means your culture doesn't offer full respect and participation to a range of diverse people and styles. Your culture doesn't yet enable all employees to participate fully. A diverse workforce needs this culture of inclusion to thrive. To see where you stand on this score, you'll need to look through the eyes of someone who is part of a non-dominant group in your organization. If you are a member of the dominant group, it can be hard to see the signs of exclusion and disrespect. Those behaviors generally will not be directed toward you and they are often inadvertent and subtle.

Here's an example where I inadvertently excluded a person with a disability from an important dialogue. I was facilitating a strategic retreat for a board of directors. With more than twenty people in a lively discussion, I was moderating by recognizing those who raised their hands. Nothing unusual there. John, one of the guests participating in this session, did not have fully functional arms. When John lifted his hand, it extended only to about shoulder level. I didn't notice his raised hand. Fortunately, a woman behind him caught my attention. I felt bad that I hadn't noticed. After that, I adjusted my focus to ensure that I would see John's raised hand.

Otherwise, my facilitation would have inadvertently excluded John from the conversation. That certainly wasn't my intent, and with my improved awareness, I quickly changed my behavior.

Not all behaviors that exclude are so easy to recognize and correct. In 2006, I had the opportunity to attend a panel discussion of eight CEOs of major corporations whose policies have been recognized as supporting diversity. At various points in the discussion, each mentioned his (all but one were men) chief diversity officer (CDO) by name. They consistently used both first and last name, conveying the respect due to a peer in a public forum, with one notable exception. One CEO mentioned his female CDO three times, each time only by her first name. When this CEO mentioned his male vice president of human resources, he used both first and last names. It's a small thing. I doubt he consciously intended disrespect, but many members of the audience felt that simple action conveyed a lower status or respect for the female CDO.

These two examples give you a sense of what a culture of inclusion means by showing you what the absence of inclusion looks like. Exclusion is generally subtle, not glaring and overt. A culture of inclusion is always important, but it is essential when you have a diverse workforce. Without it, you won't reap the benefits of diversity. Diversity without inclusion can be disruptive, leaving employees feeling uncomfortable and disconnected from each other. The differences can seem too challenging to bridge. Instead of enriching the organization, diversity can become a barrier to success. In *Mad Dogs, Dreamers and Sages*, Stephen Zades and Jane Stephens note, "The truth is that all of us have a preservational instinct towards tribalism. We are living in an era of cataclysmic change and our tendency is to insulate. When we feel uncertain, we tend to narrow our language and live in tighter realities." Zades and Stephens go on to talk about the ways that these "tighter realities" foster exclusion, not inclusion, and work against our very survival.

Without a culture of inclusion, your attempts to create a workforce that mirrors your market are doomed to fail. Either people will leave, or the organization will become fragmented and unproductive. Provide a culture of inclusion and you gain creativity and innovation, facilitating positive change.

Teaching Your Gorilla Inclusion

Creating a culture of inclusion requires much more than policy changes. Because the Gorilla is always alert to inconsistencies between policies and actions, behaviors must change too. Here are three habits you can develop to make your culture more inclusive.

Focus on the Merits of the Case: Be sure your team considers each idea on its own merits. When there is a heated debate over an issue, some people's opinions are usually more persuasive than others, partially because of the merits of the facts and logic offered and partially because of who said it. Women and minorities often report that their ideas are ignored until a member of the dominant group repeats the idea as if it were his own. The idea then becomes part of the debate.

One of the insidious habits of exclusion and disrespect is allowing the source of the idea to matter more than the idea. While this may sometimes have a logical basis, for example, the speaker's prior experience or training, it is often more related to who is in the in-crowd. It's usually unconscious. Members of the dominant group are accustomed to one another's thinking styles and communication patterns, but perhaps not to those of members of non-dominant groups. This may be compounded by the fact that different groups have different norms with regard to the pace of the conversation and the use of silence as well as other patterns. If members of the dominant group simply continue the conversation in their usual ways, other team members may feel excluded and disrespected, and their ideas may not be heard or seriously considered.

This exclusion hinders the team's performance in two ways. First, there is the obvious consequence that the idea that went unspoken or unheard might have been an important element of the solution. Second, the person who was excluded from the conversation is likely to feel less and less part of the team as this scene is repeated. The team suffers the one-time loss of a useful component for its creativity and the ongoing loss of the commitment and enthusiasm of one of its members.

Key Behavior:
Consider all ideas on their merits, not who originated the idea.

Learn to listen for communication patterns that don't fit the group's usual style and make a space for those ideas to be heard. You may need to develop your facilitation skills to help the team learn to include a variety of communication styles. Do whatever is necessary so your team can benefit from everyone's ideas and everyone can feel included in the conversation.

Surface Hidden Conflict: Conflict is a vital creative force with many dimensions. So far, we've looked at conflict in several ways. In Chapter 3, *Question Rigorously*, we examined the necessity for conflict and the need to attack issues, not people. In the preceding section of this chapter, we saw the importance of weighing the merits of the argument over its source. In Chapter 5, we will explore the role of conflict in creating commitments that produce action. In all of those cases, we were looking at differences of opinion about the issue at hand.

There is a different kind of conflict you need to consider as you work to make your culture more inclusive. To remove the real barriers to inclusion, you need to look for the unspoken conflicts between different assumptions and worldviews. These unspoken conflicts must be taken personally if we are to enable each person to contribute to her full potential. What is at issue in these conflicts is one's internalized sense of how the world works.

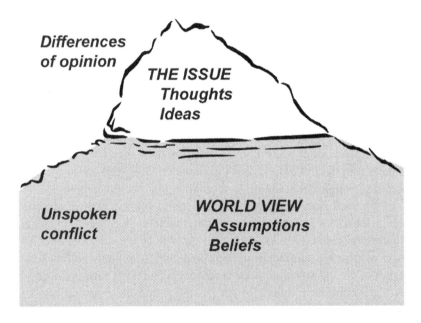

The western region of a large manufacturing company had recently been experiencing increased turnover. As the senior staff met to explore the problem, the exchange of ideas and opinions was rapid fire. Dominique, the vice president of sales, was concerned about the impact on customers and took an active role in the discussion. The director of services, Shen, didn't say much. As the group left the room for a break, Dominique approached Shen.

"How come you were so quiet in there?" she asked. "Aren't you concerned about this issue?"

Shen paused for a moment and replied, "Yes, I'm concerned. But there is never a space to speak."

Dominique smiled and said, "Yes, it's just like family dinners at my house."

Dominique and Shen had just surfaced an important, but usually unspoken, conflict. Shen's conversational patterns were different from Dominique's. Most likely, they each had assumptions and beliefs about what was happening in the meeting.

Key Behavior:
When unspoken beliefs collide, actively engage
in open exploration and dialogue.

The typical advice given to someone like Shen, who doesn't want to interrupt others to insert his ideas, is that he needs to learn to jump into the conversation. To build a truly inclusive culture, more personal exploration of this issue is needed. What if Shen and Dominique could talk more about how this conversational rhythm affects each of them, exploring their beliefs about what it means when there is silence, when someone interrupts, and other norms of communication? This would allow each of them to hear the other's stories and see each other in their own cultural context. It would offer each a window into the other's reality that would have far more impact than a cultural competence course. It might enable each of them to see the other's worldview as simply a view, not the world, and to be affected by the other's views.

Hewitt Associates uses cross-cultural learning partners to create opportunities for this sort of dialogue. Top leaders in the company are assigned cross-cultural learning partners for a one-year period. They get a personal experience with someone whose cultural background is different from theirs. It is an opportunity for each to see the other's worldview up close and personal. Absent these opportunities for dialogue, the exchange about differences is often superficial, leaving both parties mostly unchanged. Or there is no exchange at all and Shen may think that Dominique is rude whereas Dominique may think that Shen either doesn't care about the issue or doesn't have anything worthwhile to say.

These dialogues also open the door to a more trusting relationship. When you are genuinely interested in understanding a colleague's experiences and how they shape his interactions, he feels more accepted and understood. This meeting of two real human beings takes you beyond your roles in the organization. You develop a foundation for trust.

Engage Marginalized Voices: Think about the people in your organization whose collaboration is important to the organization's success. Most likely, you are more comfortable with some people than others. That's natural. If you're more comfortable with them, you're more likely to stop by their desks and chat or ask them to join you for lunch. By reaching out in those same ways to those with whom you are less comfortable, you make it easier for them to participate fully. You help them move away from the margins of the organization and into the center of things.

Work gets done through relationships. Ideas are exchanged, feedback is given, and help is offered. The invisible fabric of relationships is an essential factor in your organization's functioning. Some of those relationships happen spontaneously; others need more support. We tend to more easily trust those who are more like us. When you consciously build a bridge to employees who are different from you through casual social contact, you create a link that can help build trust in the organization. By helping an employee who might otherwise be an outsider develop her role in the relationship fabric, you strengthen the entire fabric.

Key Behavior:
Consciously use casual social time to strengthen relationships among all members of the organization.

Assumptions That Undermine Inclusion

If these behaviors of disrespect and exclusion are unintentional, why do they linger once we know they are not good for business? Some people believe the dominant group, consciously or unconsciously, is loathe to surrender its dominant position. There is likely some truth to that explanation for some of the people some of the time. More often, it may simply be a lack of awareness. In the earlier facilitation example, in which I failed to create a fully inclusive discussion, I changed my behavior when it was brought into my awareness. Some behavior habits are harder to change than others, but awareness can be a powerful tool for change.

At a deeper level, when the culture has pervasive patterns of exclusion or disrespect, shared assumptions may be blocking a more inclusive culture. These assumptions can be hard to see. For the most part, we don't think of them as assumptions but simply as "how things are." The assumptions are part of our worldview.

Three assumptions are barriers to a culture of inclusion. In each of these areas, we are seeing signs of a shift in society at large, but we still have a long way to go.

The Party Stays the Same: The dominant group often assumes that inclusion means simply inviting "the others" to participate without changing anything else. In the 1970s, as women entered the professional ranks of the workforce in unprecedented numbers, many of us adopted the mini-man model. Our approach to our differences was to mimic the dominant group—men. We wore suits in dark, neutral tones (with floppy pink ties); we talked about sports; we adopted more aggressive communication styles. The belief was that you had to be "one of the guys" if you wanted to succeed. The workplace had only one model for professional behavior, and it was a masculine model. Being feminine meant you were probably a secretary. Not a very inclusive culture.

Making special rules for special people also doesn't create inclusion. In fact, it can serve to sanction the exclusion. True inclusion comes when the culture and practices that are considered normal truly reflect everyone in the workplace. Instead of assimilating non-dominant groups into the patterns of the dominant group, the overall pattern shifts to include new behaviors and styles. Instead of inviting "the others" to the party but expecting the party to stay the same, there is an expectation that the diversity of those at the party will change the party. This is a very different assumption, and it makes for a very different party.

There Is Only One Right Answer: The belief that there is one right answer to a given problem is also a barrier to building a culture of inclusion. In problems involving people and their behavior (customers, employees, suppliers, competitors, and so forth), there is rarely only one right answer. The belief in one right answer operates unconsciously to legitimize the dominant voice and silence other voices. People who think differently or communicate differently are less likely to be heard when the "one right answer" assumption is shaping the conversation. Alternate ways of perceiving and knowing are ignored.

Key Behavior:
Look for differences of opinion eagerly; treat them as signs
that there are many right answers.

Power Is Never Discussed: An acceptance, often backed by a lack of awareness, of the unequal distribution of power serves to undermine inclusion. An awareness of the impact of power on relationships and a willingness to discuss it can help facilitate more inclusive behaviors.

When my daughter was born, my husband and I decided it would be nice for me to quit work for a while. Financially, we could handle it. But, having been employed since I was sixteen, I was accustomed to the more equal distribution of power that having two incomes encouraged. My husband couldn't understand and didn't want to discuss the ways that my lack of income might affect the way we shared power in our relationship. The power did shift and each time I raised the question, his response was to deny that anything had changed. We had slipped back toward the model we both grew up with, in which the husband assumes more control over finances. We didn't look at the changes in our relationship. At the time, I didn't fully understand why this was so upsetting to me. Later, I saw that his insistence that there was no issue felt to me like he was saying that my experience wasn't real. That is, in his mind it didn't count.

When the dominant group is unwilling to acknowledge the role of power in workplace relationships, it serves to deny the voice and reality of the non-dominant group. It excludes the non-dominant group from full participation. It denies them emotional recognition, the most fundamental foundation of inclusion and respect. It diminishes trust. If you aren't even willing to allow the topic of power into the conversation, those who are less powerful and not part of the dominant group don't feel like full participants. How are they to trust someone who acts as if a significant component of their experience doesn't exist or isn't worth talking about?

Key Behavior:
Bring the distribution of power into organizational conversations.

The assumptions we have just discussed are not easily accessible for change, either individually or organizationally. Changing how we think and challenging our basic assumptions is not simple work. Simply becoming aware of the fact that different people perceive reality differently and developing an understanding and respect for these different realities is a starting point. Without that recognition, policies and procedures to support diversity and inclusion are a hollow façade.

Three Reasons Not to Create a Culture of Inclusion

Let's get real here. After reading this chapter, you may be thinking, "But we really don't have to do this." Let's look at the three arguments most often used to support that position.

We've Always Done It This Way, and It's Worked Fine: Perhaps it has. As Ed McCracken, CEO of Silicon Graphics, Inc., was fond of saying in the 1990s, "What got us here won't get us there." Globalization isn't going to go away. Multiculturalism and other dimensions of the diverse workforce are here to stay. If you want to succeed, what you've "always done" may need to change.

These Issues Make People Uncomfortable: Right—they do. And if your culture isn't inclusive, it likely makes those who are in some way different from the dominant group feel even more uncomfortable. To move from that state to a culture of inclusion, you need to pass through the uncomfortable place called change. As a leader, that's not new territory for you. Step up to this issue and take your Gorilla forward into truly inclusive behaviors.

We Shouldn't Have to Go Out Of Our Way to Make Certain People Feel Included: This is the heavy hitter. It appears to provide a logical basis for ignoring the challenges of inclusion. Taken at face value, it's true. But this is not what this chapter advocates. I want you to go out of your way to see the ways your behavior excludes others and stop doing those things. No, this isn't just semantics. It's a different mindset. Try it on.

C-level Teams

As I write this in 2007, C-level teams are still predominantly white male. Here are a few statistics from current business websites:

- Only 21 of the Fortune 1000 CEOs are women.
- African Americans hold less than 1 percent of senior level positions in the Fortune 1000.
- Hispanics hold less than 2 percent of Fortune 1000 board seats.

If you are a C-level executive, look around the room at your next executive staff meeting. Do these statistics reflect your reality?

If they do, understanding the barriers to inclusion may be a special challenge for your team. The "white male club" in the C-suite means that at best your team has only a few members (or possibly none) who have personal experience with the subtle forms of exclusion that need to be eliminated from your organization. It will be harder for your team to see these behaviors because they aren't aimed at you. You'll need to go out of your way to see this situation through the eyes of those who have been marginalized in your organization. Listen closely to the people of color, women, people with disabilities, and others who may have been inadvertently ignored or excluded. Not because you owe it to them or because they might sue you, but because you'll learn a lot about inclusion in your organization by listening to them and looking at your organization through their eyes.

The Bottom Line

When each employee feels valued and respected, each will contribute to the organization at her fullest potential. To create such a workplace, you must look at your organization in a different way, ask yourself and your team some new questions, and create a dialogue that enables new solutions. This is much more challenging than simply shifting the membership of your organization so you have a diverse workforce. However, the rewards are substantial. By making your culture truly inclusive, you will breathe new life and vitality into your organization. You'll enhance creativity and innovation. More positive relationships among your staff will create new opportunities for collaboration. And you'll be more in tune with your market.

Action Plan:

Include Respectfully

- Consider all ideas on their merits, not who originated the idea.
- When unspoken beliefs collide, actively engage in open exploration and dialogue.
- Consciously use casual social time to strengthen relationships among all members of the organization.
- Look for differences of opinion eagerly; treat them as signs that there are many right answers.
- Bring the distribution of power into organizational conversations.

CHAPTER 5

COMMIT RESPONSIBLY

When there are two adult males in a gorilla group, the more senior of the two is the group leader and the other often serves as a sentry, bringing up the rear as the group travels or keeping watch during day-rest periods. Digit was the sentry in Uncle Bert's group. One bright December day, six poachers attacked the group. Digit charged the poachers and fought with all he had. Most of the group, including Digit's mate and unborn child, escaped. Digit took five spear wounds before he died.

Gorillas in the Mist

Digit understood not only what he was supposed to do but also why. His commitment to his task was total and absolute. Most of you aren't asking your team members for that level of commitment. However, you do need rock-solid commitments.

Commitments are the stuff of good results. Without a solid commitment from the team, you simply can't get superior results. Does this mean everyone has to agree with everything? No! So what is commitment? Let's start with a basic dictionary definition: "the state of being bound emotionally or intellectually to a course of action." The link between commitment and action starts right here with the definition. Being committed to something means you will act.

When Tandem Computers was a relatively young company and the quality movement was gaining momentum in the United States, Jim Treybig, Tandem founder and then-CEO, came to a meeting of Tandem's new group of quality assurance professionals. In his down-home Texas style, he said to the group, "Don't just be involved; be committed. Does anybody know the difference? When you have bacon and eggs for breakfast, the pig—he was committed. The chicken was just involved."

The group laughed, but we understood Treybig's meaning. He was imploring those of us on the quality team to put our all into this effort. He wanted us to be emotionally and intellectually bound to a course of action.

Let's look at the five elements of a solid commitment. Every commitment needs who, what, when, why, and how.

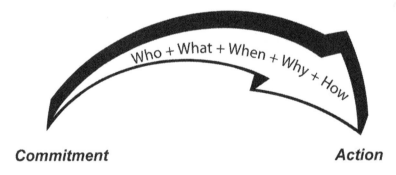

Commitment   **Action**

John's small IT company was struggling to grow fast enough to satisfy its investors. The company was working on two different products and actively pursuing customers for both. While the two products relied on the same core technologies, each required separate development, marketing, and sales efforts. As the founder and CEO, John felt the company had to decide whether to continue to pursue both options, thus spreading the risk, or put all its eggs in one basket to more effectively focus their efforts. A case could be made for each side of the argument.

As vice president of sales, Chris argued that two products would provide more traction in the market than one. From her perspective as data center director, Lizzie saw it differently. She believed the ability to scale cost-effectively was essential to satisfying the investors and that focusing on one product would make that possible. She also argued that as a small company, focus was more important than reach. The analysis and discussions went round and round.

Finally, the management team decided to focus all of the company's energies in one direction, abandoning one product to pursue the other more aggressively. Not long after that, Chris dedicated some resources to the pursuit of an opportunity for the discontinued product, and Joachim, the development director, allowed development work to continue on the discontinued product. What happened here?

Who, What, and When

The team made a decision and a commitment to act on it. However, execution of that decision was seriously flawed. Let's start by looking at the *who* and *what* of the commitment. The *who* was each individual member of the team, not the entire team. Identifying the team as the owner of the commitment removed responsibility from each individual and invited ambiguity in the what. In this case, the *what* was for each member of the executive team to allocate resources to pursuing only one of the products. Chris and Joachim acted on this in a different way than other team members did. The decision didn't stick. The *what* of this commitment was also poorly defined. The team made a decision to focus on one product, but they didn't discuss what that meant in terms of following up sales leads for the other product. With an ambiguous *what*, there is too much room for differences in interpretation of the commitment.

For Joachim, *when* was the problem. He was planning to phase out work on the discontinued product after the current research projects had been completed. Because this work was leading-edge technology that was significant to the company in the long run, Joachim felt it would be a waste to throw away the progress his team had made by abandoning the efforts in the midst of the current development.

Because John and his team often neglected some combination of the *who*, *what*, and *when*, they frequently had difficulty getting decisions to stick. They wasted a lot of time by frequently making the same decision. By getting clear agreements about the *who*, *what*, and *when* of their commitments, they could have prevented this problem. Instead, each time a decision failed to stick, it added one more story to the Gorilla's Guide showing that it wasn't important to *commit responsibly* .

The *what* sometimes needs further clarification. If the commitment is a soft item, you may need to specify how you will know it when you see it. Some people talk about metrics for commitments, but this may lead you down the wrong path. It's not just about the numbers. For example, when you've made a hard decision in which there was significant disagreement, you may need to talk about what it means to support the decision. Or if engineering agreed to help marketing with the rollout, team members need to know what that looks like so they will know when the commitment has been met.

How

Marisa's executive team had mastered the *who*, *what*, and *when* of commitment. They also took time to *question rigorously*. As a result, they generally made high-quality decisions quickly. Team members were truly committed. Their issue was the *how*. Asking how is the link between the decision and accountability for action. Without asking how, members of Marisa's team found it difficult to hold each other accountable. They didn't have the information they needed for good follow-up and accountability.

When your team makes an important decision, the execution will often involve a stretch goal for at least one team member. Many teams allow the discussion to end when that team member commits to the stretch goal. But that's when they need to start asking *how*. Without a clear sense of how the goal will be met, it's difficult for team members to be fully engaged in supporting the stretch goal or hold the primary owner accountable. I'm not talking about getting down in the weeds or trying to manage each other's activities. I am suggesting that a shared understanding of how a challenging target will be met can help your team avoid disasters and create more accountability.

If the commitment is a big stretch or the owner of the commitment is new to the role, including *what if* in your *how* will further strengthen the commitment. What if you're unable to get our partner company to agree? What if the supplier quality is substandard? For a challenging goal, the responsible team member may need the team's help in thinking through what could go wrong. Rather than letting that team member be surprised and then let the team down, think through things as a team.

Key Behavior:
Hold each other accountable as peers.
Don't let the boss get stuck with this job!

Why

To understand the importance of *why*, let's talk about worms. Worms? Here's the deal. Back in the 1970s (when psychology professors had fewer constraints on using their students as guinea pigs), some professors experimented with what it would take to convince students to eat worms. Yes, real earth worms. (There are several such studies. See, for example, Foxman, 1970.)

It turns out that *why* was a pivotal factor. When the task was framed in the context of a lofty goal, the students were much more likely to agree to eat the worm. They either reframed the task or modified their self-perception. When students were told that the worm-eating project would make an important contribution to research that would help mankind, some changed their conception of the task. They were no longer doing something gross; they were doing something significant. Other students redefined themselves. Instead of being an undergraduate guinea pig, they came to see themselves as courageous enough to do something others might not do. Students who didn't reconceptualize either the task or themselves were less likely to eat the worms.

The strength of the commitments in your team depends on the strength of the *why*. Are you committing to eat worms or are you committing to help mankind?

Presumably you aren't asking your employees to eat worms or perform other gross and pointless acts. But you do need their discretionary effort, that additional measure of persistence and creativity that goes beyond doing their job. When your employees are fully engaged, you'll get their effort beyond a day's work for a day's pay. This culture of discretionary effort can make all the difference in your organization's performance.

Leslee is the administrator of a community health clinic for HIV-positive patients. Leslee noted that her nurses average about ten years of experience in working with HIV so they've seen many challenging and heart-rending situations.

When I asked her for an example of something extraordinary that someone on her staff had done, she said it was impossible for her to cite just one instance. "We see that all the time—staff members going out of their way to make sure the patients have what they need. People really do step up."

Clearly, this is a job with a high risk of burnout. But Leslee described a staff imbued with the significance of the work they are doing. They were ready to go the extra mile. They have a clear and compelling *why*.

Members of your organization may not literally be saving lives, but you can help them remember the big picture. It's easy for any of us to get caught up in the day-to-day details of our job. We forget how our work connects to what others are doing in the organization. We get focused on our goals, our work, and our deadlines. Instead, you need to constantly keep the bigger picture in front of employees. What organizational result is their project connected to? Will it help the company close a new account or create a new product? When team members see those connections, there are fewer turf wars and more discretionary effort. The level of commitment to the organization's results increases. As one company founder said simply, "Culture makes the impossible possible."

Communicating Commitments

Communication is the glue that holds your commitments together. Three communication elements must be present for *commit responsibly* to work in your organization.

Lively Debate: Every team member needs a chance to voice her opinions about any significant decision the team makes. Regardless of the issue or point of view, each person on the team should be heard.

Let's look at how this plays out in one team at Dell. Gary is in product marketing. His core team consists of employees from every function that will be impacted by decisions about his product, including sales, engineering, manufacturing, and finance. One simple decision can be a $50 million bet. Get it wrong and Dell could lose customers; get it right and sales and profits for that product could soar. Since Dell has a reputation for quick decisions, how does this team do it with so many different perspectives and goals to include?

In Gary's team, the debate is open, and it can get pretty vocal if the issue is controversial. As Gary said, "It's fine for me to say, 'This won't work,' right up until we decide." This debate is essential to getting real commitment. When team members get a chance to have their ideas heard, it's easier for them to sign up to the decision.

Several key elements make this debate work. One is the development of trust in the team and the whole organization. Team members need to feel some measure of safety in the team, so trust is important. It helps to know that the debate isn't personal. Be sure you stick to the issue instead of digressing into personality conflicts. If tempers get heated, you sometimes need to take a break. Use your own feelings as a guide. If you hear yourself talking too fast or interrupting someone, it's likely that you're getting agitated. If you are, others probably are too. Ask for a pause in the discussion, a brief moment when no one is speaking. If that doesn't seem to restore your equilibrium, maybe it's time for a break. For this lively debate to produce commitment, everyone needs to feel that his point of view has been heard. As the leader, you need to create the environment that makes that possible.

It takes time to let everyone have input into a team decision. A much faster alternative is to decree the answer and get on with it. However, if you want efficient, effective execution and an engaged, creative workforce, you need to take full advantage of all the brainpower on your team. That means that everyone's input counts. It doesn't mean you have to listen to the debate forever. When the discussion becomes circular and the ideas have all been expressed, it's time to ask, "Does anyone have data or opinions that we haven't heard yet?" This helps team members realize that it's time to decide. Sensing when the discussion has gone on long enough requires careful listening. Pay attention to whether what you are hearing is new information or a rerun of the same old story. The more attentively you listen, the easier it will be to know how long is too long.

GE has used the "fist-to-five" process for years to identify where everyone stands on an issue. This is used more to take a poll or get a sense of the room than to take a vote. The idea is simple. If you wholeheartedly endorse the proposal, you hold up five fingers. If you can barely say you'll support it, you hold up one finger. In between, there are gradations of support. If you raise a closed fist, you are indicating that you cannot live with this proposal. You are telling your colleagues that you will leave the team rather than have your name associated with the proposed action. Generally, this means the team needs to return to the discussion to be sure your concerns have been heard, lest they make a collective mistake. Perhaps further risk management strategies can be developed to reduce your concerns. Smart team members reserve the fist for issues they would truly resign over—a real line in the sand, instead of using it to hold the team hostage to a point of view. Like other consensus-building techniques, fist-to-five requires trust among team members to be useful.

Expressing the Commitment: Whatever technique you use to gain consensus, be sure that each person opts in publicly and visibly. At Dell, when the team has formulated a plan of action, each team member will literally sign the plan (electronically, that is). Once a team member approves something, she can never come back and say, "I never thought that was going to fly." As Gary put it, "I can disagree all day long. But once the core team decides, nobody tolerates reneging on your commitment. The whole team will shut you down."

Once a decision is made, it's really made. Gary summarized it this way. "This sounds corny, but we live or die together." It may sound corny, but it gets results. And the Dell Gorilla's Guide has the stories to prove it.

Key Behavior:
Voice commitments out loud.
Never let silence be your form of commitment.

The commitment can be a written approval (as we saw in the Dell example), a verbal roll call vote on the phone, or a raised hand in a meeting. As long as each person has publicly committed to the plan, members of the team can hold each other accountable for that commitment. Making commitments visible and explicit helps prevent misunderstandings and builds trust. It's a way of preventing the pocket veto in which someone remains silent and then later says he never agreed to the plan. "Pocket vetoes" destroy trust. Prevent that in your team by getting each member's explicit commitment.

Following Up on the Commitment: Your communication after the commitment can be just as important as that leading up to the commitment.

Key Behavior:
When the team makes a decision, each member of the team
supports the decision both verbally and with actions.

If your team has made a solid decision and team members are truly committed, each team member will tell others in the organization about the decision in the right way.

This isn't about being politically correct. It's about owning the decision with each team member knowing he had a time and place to voice his views and the team ultimately made a decision. Whether or not team members like the decision, they will present it as "we decided," not "they decided, but I disagree." When related decisions are made, they support the team's decision.

Team members also need to be proactive in communicating problems to the team. If it looks like you will be unable to meet your commitment, let your team know.

Key Behavior:
If you can see that it's likely you won't meet your commitment,
give your team a heads-up as early as possible.

By letting others know about issues in advance, you help establish trust. Your colleagues can rely on your commitments. Members of teams in which trust is lacking often feel as though someone is constantly looking over their shoulder. To prevent that, keep team members sufficiently informed about your progress so they develop enough trust to make extra oversight unnecessary. It's not enough to say, "They should trust me." You can help team members be more trusting by keeping them informed.

The Leader's Personal Commitment

Leaders may face several personal challenges in getting *commit responsibly* firmly embedded in the culture. If you are uncomfortable with conflict, the lively debate needed to get to a strong commitment may be challenging for you. This discomfort sometimes shows up as avoidance of conflict; it sometimes materializes as an impatience with discussion. Either way, this can be a real barrier to your success. People disagree. If you can hang in there through the discussion, the most creative solutions often come out of those disagreements. Three issues can get in your way.

If you are uncomfortable with conflict, you need to move beyond your discomfort. Conflict is a vital creative force in your organization. To get over your discomfort, you'll likely need to learn what assumptions and beliefs you have about conflict and how it may affect you. No, you don't need years of psychoanalysis, just some thoughtful reflection.

In *How the Way We Talk Can Change the Way We Work*, Robert Kegan and Lisa Lahey have designed an excellent process to help you uncover the beliefs that make it hard for you to change your behavior. At the heart of this process is the idea that we often have competing commitments that interfere with our goals. Because we are unaware of this dynamic, we can't see why we don't make progress on the goals. By helping you see your competing commitments and the hidden assumptions that drive them, Kegan and Lahey unlock the door to individual change. Using this tool will expand your options for handling conflict constructively.

If you prefer not to know when someone doesn't support your views, you also face a personal challenge with *commit responsibly*. You may believe that if the lack of support isn't allowed to surface, it will go away. Leaders who feel they can starve dissent by lack of oxygen are kidding themselves. Unexpressed dissent smolders and may eventually burst into flames. By not wanting to hear what the dissenters have to say, you cut yourself off from a valuable source of information about possible risks and alternative actions. This can be a serious handicap to your leadership, especially as you rise higher in the organization.

If you are just plain burned out, this may be the most personal challenge. Maybe you no longer care about your organization or its mission. You can't inspire the organization about the big picture of company results because you either have given up or feel it doesn't matter. You don't feel you make a difference anymore. If you find yourself in this situation, find a way to take a break. I don't mean a long weekend. If you are seriously burned out, it may take a year or more to rejuvenate and regain your perspective. For some people, it takes a job or career change. First, simply take a long, hard look at how you are feeling about your work. If the company results don't matter to you or you feel you can't make a difference in those results, find some space to reconsider how your work fits in your life and make some choices about what to do with what you learn about yourself.

C-level Teams

There are some unique challenges to *commit responsibly* in the C-level team. The CEO and her direct reports have nowhere to take their disagreements. In other teams, if team members reach an impasse and simply can't come to agreement on an important issue, the issue can be escalated through management for resolution and then integrated into the team's plan. However, in the C-level team, that would mean the CEO making the decision. While that is always an option, it's one that should be used very sparingly as it can leave team members feeling less than fully accountable. This is a problem at any level of the organization, but it's especially damaging in the C-level team. When C-level team members feel the CEO has unilaterally made the decision, it's much harder for them to hold each other accountable for the results. The CEO gets left holding the bag for accountability in the team. That breakdown ratchets down the team's power. And, the breakdown gets circulated in the Gorilla's Guide, affecting teams throughout the organization.

C-level teams also face a challenge with *commit responsibly* because each team member must be constantly looking through two different lenses. First, she must manage her piece of the business. Whether that is a function, a geographical unit, or a line of business, each member of the CEO's staff has a piece of the business to run. At the same time, collectively this team must run the entire business. Each team member must look at any given problem or decision not only in terms of how it affects her piece of the business but also in terms of how it affects the whole business. While this is true at lower levels in the organization as well, nowhere is it as critical as in the C-level team. This team must hold the big picture of the company's results for the entire organization. If they lose that focus and instead put the success of their individual organizations first, the whole company will be full of silos and fiefdoms.

Key Behavior:
Sacrifice your own personal results or those of your team
when it is necessary to achieve a company result.

Virtual Teams

Your organization will increasingly rely on virtual teams. These teams don't have frequent face-to-face contact, but they can still establish the same norms of commitment. It just takes a little extra attention. The biggest challenge can be in getting an open, constructive debate when you can't see each other. You'll need to pay special attention to developing and maintaining trust. If the debate is by phone, be sure that everyone's ideas are heard. Even with the best of intentions, it can be hard for some team members to get their ideas out in a conference call. Those with a slower or softer speech may not find a way to jump into the fray. In a heated debate or even a fast-paced conversation, you may find it helpful to pause every few minutes and check to be sure everyone has had a chance to speak.

Getting public commitment over the phone also can be difficult. If you just ask, "Is everyone okay with this plan?" two things can go wrong. First, because there is no visual cue to anchor the meaning of "this plan," you may not all have the same plan in mind. If you're using a web-based tool or other communications technology to share visuals, be sure that everyone is literally on the same page. Second, quiet dissenters may not speak up in response to your question. They disagree, but they find it easier to remain silent. Because you hear a chorus of "yes," you may not realize that you have dissenters. If the discussion has been contentious, it can be helpful to use a roll call reply. Ask each person to weigh in on the question by name. For example, "This is Gadi. I'm on board." This ensures that you hear from everyone and that everyone experiences her own public commitment to the plan.

You also may want to use a verbal version of the fist-to-five process. Ask each person on the call to voice their fist-to-five opinion. If you're using web-based collaboration software, you can also use that system to take a fist-to-five poll.

Multicultural Teams[3]

Commitments always exist within a given context. That's why we've stressed the who, when, how, and why in addition to the what of a commitment. In addition to that immediate context, commitments are also made and understood within the individual's larger cultural context. Cultures vary in the ways in which they make and execute decisions.

Some cultures, for example, Eastern European, Asian, and African, tend to defer to those in positions of authority or seniority and view the hierarchy with more respect. On the other hand, the Anglo American culture that dominates most American organizations tends to reject authority and hierarchy. As a multicultural team works to make a decision, different cultural assumptions are operating about the role of authority and hierarchy in the decision-making process. Explicitly defining your process can help the team have a more balanced discussion and reach a better decision.

In addition, cultures vary in the way they balance task and relationship in both decision-making and execution. For example, in Latino, Asian, and Native American cultures, relationship development in the early phase of the project is essential. Only after that foundation is built will the focus shift to task completion. Similarly, in Arab and Eastern European cultures, a foundation of trust and friendship is crucial. In Anglo American culture, tasks tend to take precedence over relationships. This task/relationship balance can impact how commitments are made and executed. Getting to know your team members in the context of their cultural heritage will help you execute more effectively.

The Bottom Line

How your organization handles commitments is a vital aspect of your ability to execute. Words like "empowerment" and "accountability" will come and go from your focus. Whatever the current buzzwords, commitment forms the vital link between decisions and action. If you don't manage how your culture handles that link, execution will suffer.

---

[3] *Please* remember that these are high-level, general statements about culture. All of us are affected by our cultural context, but we are also unique individuals. Use these generalizations to increase your sensitivity and awareness and provide a framework for understanding your team members, but *not* to stereotype groups or individuals.

Action Plan:
Commit Responsibly

- Hold each other accountable as peers. Don't let the boss get stuck with this job!
- Voice commitments out loud. Never let silence be your form of commitment.
- When the team makes a decision, each member of the team supports the decision both verbally and with actions.
- If you can see that it's likely you won't meet your commitment, give your team a heads-up as early as possible.
- Sacrifice your own personal results or those of your team when it is necessary to achieve a company result.

CHAPTER 6

EXPERIMENT RELENTLESSLY

Fossey was temporarily sharing her cabin with a young female gorilla, Coco, who had been captured by poachers and was near death from dehydration. She left for about an hour, expecting that Coco would remain asleep. Instead, she returned to find total chaos. "The 'gorilla-proof' matting the men had nailed over the camp's stock of food supplies, stored in shelves along one wall of Coco's room, had been torn away from the storage cupboards. In the midst of an array of tin cans and opened boxes Coco sat contentedly sampling sugar, flour, jam, rice, and spaghetti. My momentary dismay at the havoc she had created was instantly replaced with delight upon realizing that she somehow had had the curiosity and energy to create such a mess."

Gorillas in the Mist

Yes, sometimes experimentation is messy! Embrace the opportunity to experiment—not occasionally or when it's tidy but continually, relentlessly! To do that, you will need to see the outcomes of experiments as learning opportunities rather than successes or failures. A mistake is simply an experiment that didn't turn out the way you'd planned. More importantly, it's an opportunity to learn what doesn't work. If your organization is going to be innovative and stay ahead of the curve, you must experiment constantly. For employees to be willing to experiment, your Gorilla needs to view each experience as a good thing, whether it turns out the way they expected it to or not.

Not every organization works that way. When I was first out of college, I went to work for the U.S. Government as a software engineer. I joined a group of professionals who had been with the federal government for years. They understood the culture there. I was young and eager. I wanted to do the best job I possibly could. I worked really hard on the projects I was given, eager to come up with creative solutions. One of my colleagues saw what I was doing and said, "Don't get so fancy. You'll make the rest of us look bad."

Talk about an anti-innovation culture! No one experimented or colored outside the lines. The Gorilla's Guide told us to show up, plod along the well-trodden path, and go home after our eight hours.

On the other hand, consider how *experiment relentlessly* works at BookPeople, the largest independent bookstore in the United States. Steve Bercu, manager and part-owner, tells his employees, "Keep experimenting all the time. If it doesn't work, don't worry about it. We'll change it back."

As a result of this attitude, BookPeople employees have come up with some very creative ideas, including a kids' camp based on the children's books by popular author, Rick Riordan, a new idea for displaying books that increases sales, a beautiful mural in the kids' reading area, and other ideas from store décor to merchandising.

Key Behavior:
When a decision isn't producing the desired results,
try something else.

All of these innovative ideas—experiments—contribute to BookPeople's success. Some of the experiments at BookPeople were successful, others got "changed back." But none were failures. Each time, the organization learned something and became more innovative. By actively managing culture, BookPeople is thriving while many independent bookstores are losing their markets to chains and the Internet. The attitude of continual experimentation that Bercu has fostered at BookPeople translates to real bottom-line success.

Three Beliefs That Kill Experimentation

Innovation and creativity are natural, and yet the culture in many organizations contains beliefs that block the natural urge to experiment. Three are particularly problematic.

You Can't Afford To Be Seen As Having Participated In a "Failed" Experiment: This belief can make your organization end up like the federal government workforce with a stodgy reputation and little innovation. This belief breeds a C.Y.A (Cover Your Arse) mentality, which will make experimentation an outlaw in your organization. You know the symptoms. Instead of trying to figure out what can be learned from a problem, everyone is busy trying to show that the problem isn't his fault. Instead of talking about the merit of an idea, people talk about who will or won't like it. Politics as usual, right?

Wrong. It's the death knell of both effective execution and innovation. If C.Y.A. is a prevalent pattern in your culture, then you can pretty well guarantee that employees are wasting time. Every minute an employee spends covering their backside is a minute that could have been spent serving your customers or developing your products. How can you possibly execute effectively with time and energy being wasted that way? Also, since experimentation and the protective, defensive mindset of C.Y.A. are extreme enemies, you're not likely to find them in the same culture. Experimentation is crucial to innovation, so if you have C.Y.A. stories in your Gorilla's Guide, they've got to go!

When team members are afraid to be associated with mistakes, it can engender a lack of ownership of results. Consider this episode from a large community nonprofit organization. Every spring, the organization runs a season-specific fund-raising campaign. The slogan has been the same for years, and it's been quite successful. People love it and remember it. This year, Doug, the vice president of marketing, decided it was time for a change. He had managed the campaign with the old slogan several times, and he was bored with it. He figured that others must be feeling the same way, so he created a totally new message for this year's campaign. This could have been a productive learning experiment for the organization. As it turned out, the campaign was far less successful than in prior years. Instead of making it a learning opportunity, Doug played C.Y.A. He focused his attention only on his perception that the other groups didn't do their part to make the campaign a success. He didn't look at what the organization might learn from the experiment. In fact, he didn't view it as an experiment at all. Instead of making this a productive experience, Doug simply denied ownership of the results. Learning and innovation lost the battle to protectiveness. And the organization lost a valuable opportunity to learn.

It's an old, but true, story. From 1878 to 1880, Thomas Edison and his associates worked on at least 3,000 different theories to create an efficient incandescent light. Without a willingness to experiment, make mistakes, and learn from them, innovation in almost any arena is almost impossible. Mistakes are a tremendous organizational resource. Don't waste them!

Mistakes Are Embarrassing: Do you see experiments that produce unexpected results as something to celebrate, tolerate, or eliminate? For most of us, it's eliminate or, at best, tolerate. And the cultural norms in the organization reflect that bias.

The process of growing up and getting an education left most of us with a few bumps and bruises. The well-intentioned actions of parents and teachers often taught us that mistakes are something to be ashamed of. In my high school chemistry class, Beth mixed the wrong chemicals together in the lab experiment and created a small explosion. Cool! Well, that was my reaction anyway. But Mr. Masterson lectured Beth about the need to read the instructions more carefully. She was embarrassed and ashamed as the teacher publicly bemoaned her mistake.

Since we were all paying close attention at that moment and were very emotionally engaged, Mr. Masterson missed a big teaching opportunity. What if he had focused on what we could learn about the nature of those two chemicals from this accidental experiment? He surely had our undivided attention! That lesson would have stuck. We would have seen a great example of the learning inherent in even an accidental experiment. Instead, we learned that failed experiments are a source of shame and embarrassment.

Think about watching a child take its first steps. We applaud every effort. We don't stand there saying, "Wow, I can't believe she did that. What a dumb way to do it." We know she will make many false starts before she really takes off. And we applaud each one as part of the learning process. We see each experiment as a necessary part of the journey to success.

Needless to say, most of us have a lot more experiences like Beth's chemistry class explosion, when we have felt ashamed or embarrassed. We don't have a lot of experience with experiments being applauded as part of the path to success.

During a strategy session with the executive team of a regional retail group, Alexandra talked about a recent project. She labeled it as a failure.

Other team members immediately asked her why she called it a failure, explaining that they saw it as a learning experience for the team. Alexandra replied, "I get that it wasn't a failure to you. But I have failed myself." She could see that her personal life experience was causing her to see this as a failure even though the rest of the team didn't see it that way.

It takes powerful directives in the Gorilla's Guide to overcome our personal life messages about failures and mistakes. Your culture must have enough positive messages about experimenting and learning that employees can see experiments as valuable opportunities to learn and exciting evidence of innovation, not personal failures.

What People Think Matters More Than the Results You Get: This belief is a bit of a sleeper. It probably isn't something that would concern you if you noticed it in your organization. Still, it's a significant barrier to experimentation. When someone floats a new idea, do people tend to ask "What do you think Alberto will say?" or "Let's think about how Eliza will react."? If that sort of conversation is commonplace, your organization is missing opportunities to learn.

The unspoken assumption behind these questions is that an individual's reaction to the idea is more essential than an open dialogue in which everyone can learn. Experimentation is discouraged; opportunities for both innovation and learning may be lost. Sometimes these conversations are used to explore an idea more thoroughly and improve on it before sharing it more widely. That's great. But all too often, these comments indicate that the organization's decision-making is distorted by what Art Kleiner called the "core group" and their opinions.

In *Who Really Matters*, Kleiner pointed out that whatever an organization's mission or goals may be, it "is continually acting to fulfill the perceived needs and priorities of its core group." While attention to the core group's needs is a source of energy and direction, it's also one of the invisible forces that can block experimentation and learning. Members of the core group may or may not have official authority but what people think they want shapes behavior. Before you decide whether you should kiss up to the core group or try to overthrow them, get Kleiner's book and go straight to Chapter Twenty Three. It will help you avoid significant pain and frustration.

Unintended Consequences and Other Enemies

It's unlikely that anyone in your organization sat in a conference room on a Friday afternoon and said, "Let's set things up so no one will ever want to experiment with doing anything new." Most of these barriers to experimentation are the unintended consequences of other strategies or actions. More than likely, your systems and processes were set up to encourage reasonable goals such as predictability or loyalty. But the unintended consequence may be a C.Y.A. or a risk-averse organization. For example, an organization that values predictability may reward managers whose units perform according to plan. In doing so, it may discourage the experimentation and innovation that could make things less predictable in the short term but more profitable in the long term.

Many organizations have a practice of promoting only those managers who haven't had any visible failures. A manager who wants to rise in such an organization must either hide his failures or refuse to take risks. Either approach undermines experimentation. These promotion practices may be well-documented official policies or they may simply reflect the unconscious preferences of senior management. Because promotions tell the organization what behavior is valued, these promotion practices fill the Gorilla's Guide with messages that it's important to avoid visible failures. They pack a triple punch. If the policy is official, it's part of Track 1 (official messages). In addition, these stories are usually popular on the grapevine and become part of Track 2 (events). Finally, employees' interpretations of who is promoted and why become part of Track 3 (interpretations). Instead of a culture that values experimentation as a source of learning, you get a culture that avoids mistakes at all costs. Not a great way to encourage innovation!

To fight this risk-averse mindset, you need to let your own mistakes and learning experiences be visible. Be an open, eager learner. Let the organization see how that contributes to success. Recognize and promote learning and experimentation.

Key Behavior:
Acknowledge your mistakes;
be open about what you learned from them.

By acknowledging your mistakes, you also build trust in the organization. People see that you are being honest with yourself and with them about what happened. The shadow of an unacknowledged mistake can lead people to doubt your willingness to play straight with them.

The new vice president of strategic planning at a large bank botched his first planning cycle pretty badly. Paul had come from a very hierarchical, command and control organization. Somewhat predictably, he failed to make the planning process participatory. Members of the planning team felt frustrated and disempowered. During the next planning cycle, Paul made sure to design the process to include much more participation. He asked for input about the process, timing of meetings, and the strategy itself. The staff loved the new process. About halfway through the cycle, Paul opened the planning team meeting by acknowledging that he had made a mistake the previous year by not creating a participatory process. The team already knew that and had seen that he had learned from his mistake. But, as one team member put it, "By admitting that in front of all twenty-five of us, Paul scored big. He showed us his vulnerability. Trust took a giant leap up."

Organizational inertia blocks risk taking and the honest assessment of risks and results that fosters learning. Carly Fiorina, the former CEO of Hewlett-Packard, recounted her experiences of being told, "That's not how we do it here" in *Tough Choices*. Fiorina's style was more direct and aggressive than Hewlett-Packard's employees were accustomed to. She needed to make some changes in the organization to make Hewlett-Packard more successful. However, the organizational inertia exhibited in the frequent remarks of "That's not how we do it here" blocked the organization's ability to experiment, learn, and adapt.

Key Behavior:
Seek out opportunities to experiment with doing things differently;
recognize the learning opportunities inherent in the change.

It's on the Agenda

There are three patterns in organizations that *experiment relentlessly*.

Learning Is on the Agenda: In organizations that *experiment relentlessly*, learning is a core process. Leaders seize opportunities to have conversations about what can be learned in staff meetings, project debriefs, hallway conversations, and so forth. They build learning into the formal processes.

Start with your process for considering new ideas. Begin to ask about learning opportunities when a decision is still being discussed. Instead of focusing only on success or failure, focus on the experiment by asking, "What will we learn from this?" This question broadens the definition of success to include learning. You may find it useful to use this question in several different conversations as you consider innovative ideas. The point is not that you don't care whether the plan works. The point is that whether the plan works or not, you want the team to be in a learning mindset, looking for opportunities to experiment and learn from the start of the project. This signals that you value the experimentation, regardless of the outcome.

To reinforce the message that learning matters to you, institute post-action review and mid-action review processes. To foster a mindset of experimentation, the review must:

(1) Occur very soon after the action. In a fairly tactical environment, the review should occur within a few hours or days. For a larger project, conduct mini-debriefs as each phase of the project is completed. These mini-debriefs, or mid-action reviews, allow you to incorporate your learning as you continue with the project. This provides immediate payoff for the time invested.

(2) Focus on learning, not blame or reward. This is hard, and your culture may not support this mindset. The point is not to lay credit or blame at someone's feet but for everyone to use the experience to develop new insights about the business or the customers or their own skills, attitudes, or actions. This doesn't mean that the responsible person is off the hook. If someone has dropped the ball, he needs to answer to the team for his failure to deliver. Still, the focus should be primarily on learning, not on flaying the guilty party.

(3) Happen consistently. Whether the action was deemed a success or failure, there is something to be learned in a post-action or mid-action review.

Most leaders know they need to do a post-action review, but few consistently use these three principles of successful learning debriefs.

A good learning debrief helps participants close the experiential learning loop, linking action and reflection. Terry Borton's model in *Reach,*

Touch and Teach is one of the most practical.

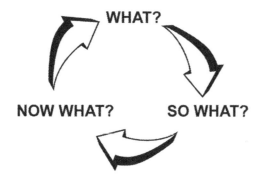

Your learning debrief should include both *so what* and *now what*. In *so what*, participants reflect on their experience to gain new ideas or insights. In *now what*, participants have an opportunity to decide what to do with what they have learned. Deciding how to apply the insights from this project leads back to *what*. In *what*, participants actively use their learning and begin the cycle again.[4]

When a large global manufacturing company upgraded to a new system for order processing and demand management, it required a team of almost one hundred people working for more than two years to fully implement the new system. Jorge had been with the company for seven years when he was tapped to lead this effort. His team members had been on loan from their organizations. By the time the project ended, they had practically forgotten what their old jobs were. Jorge knew that both the individuals and the company would benefit from a systematic retrospective on the project.

We planned a daylong event for the extended leadership team of about twenty people, designed to surface and highlight both personal and organizational learning. The team spent the day looking back over the two years they had spent on the project. They drew a timeline, shared stories, looked for patterns in their experiences, and extracted valuable lessons learned. At the end of the day, several "ah-ha's" had developed. The individual team members were ready to take what they had learned and go on to the next

---

[4] To learn more about how to apply this model with your team, visit www.FourthFactorOnline.com under Resources.

assignment. Jorge had several gems of insight that he planned to apply to the ongoing operation of the system.

Key Behavior:
Build learning into your business processes.

If you want to take *experiment relentlessly* to the extreme, follow the lead of some executives who are experimenting with intentional mistakes. By identifying key assumptions and designing actions that will fail if those assumptions are true, managers can learn more and learn faster. For example, smart advertising agencies may deliberately include ads they think won't work in a campaign. This allows them to test their assumptions about the market and innovate more successfully. It's important that these be experiments where the benefit of testing the assumption outweighs the risk of the possible failure. That makes it a safe, manageable risk.

Early Warning Signs Are Thoughtfully Examined: As a leader, you set the tone for what happens when it looks like things aren't turning out the way you'd like them to. You may find it more comfortable to ignore the early warning signs and stay the course. Bringing the evidence that things aren't on track out into the open can feel threatening. Your failure might be exposed. However, if you want to have a culture that supports experimentation and innovation, you need to create an open dialogue about those early warning signs. What are you seeing? Do others interpret the evidence the same way you do? What options do you have? How would you know if it was time to change directions? All of these questions will help you react more quickly to things turning out differently than you had planned. And, if these conversations are a routine event, experimentation is more likely to prevail in your organization.

When something bothers or frustrates you, what do you do? Maybe you ignore it and go around the problem. Perhaps like one CEO, you simply walk away when someone approaches you with a problem! Not a good idea if you want experimentation and innovation in your culture. When you skirt around a problem, you support the idea that problems are embarrassing or difficult to handle. You miss an opportunity to signal that a problem is really a learning opportunity, something to be valued, not something to be avoided.

You also undermine trust. If you totally ignore the issue, people lose faith in your willingness to engage with challenges. If you deal with the problem indirectly, by talking to someone other than the person responsible, you convey the message that talking about someone rather than to her is acceptable. Avoiding direct engagement creates an atmosphere of politics and innuendo, not trust.

Cheri managed the order processing group for a West Coast manufacturing company. She had joined the company straight out of college and had been promoted rapidly to supervisor and then manager. Cheri still struggled to earn respect from some of her older colleagues. On a fairly regular basis, Gerald, the vice president of manufacturing, neglected to pass important information along to Cheri's group in a timely way. Being young and inexperienced, Cheri would march over to her boss' office and tell him what Gerald had done. Cheri's boss would pick up the phone and call Gerald. "Hey, Gerald, would you come to my office for a minute?" Then Cheri would talk to Gerald about the issue face-to-face in her boss' office. After a couple of rounds of this awkward process, Cheri learned her lesson—go directly to the person with whom you have an issue.

Cheri's boss refused to let her be part of what I call "bitch and run." She learned to address problems in a direct way with a focus on learning, not blame. Her boss' insistence on handling the problem directly was a strong signal that the desire to learn overrides the challenges of dealing with problems.

Key Behavior:
Deal directly with things that don't work. Don't bitch and run.

On the flip side, if you go on the attack when there is a problem, you risk signaling that learning is less important than blaming. The middle ground—collaboratively exploring the problem and its causes and cures—is where you can get your culture to embrace experimentation.

The combination of open dialogue and dealing directly with issues will help your culture value learning and experimentation. As we discussed in Chapter 3, it will also help you *question rigorously*.

Passion Overrides Fear: One way to overcome individual fears about the embarrassment associated with mistakes is to instill a passion so powerful that it overrides the fear. The vice president described earlier, who labeled her project a failure, did not allow her disappointment or shame at failing to stop her from experimenting and innovating and learning. Why? She passionately believes in the organization's mission. Perhaps more importantly, she sees the link between her work and that mission. Her passion overrides her fears.

The commitment and passion for the organization's work is a key element. Remember, the Gorilla's Guide must have messages about experimentation and risk-taking that are so strong that they will overcome our fears of being shamed or embarrassed by our mistakes. Our sense of pride in the organization and its accomplishments has to help us rise above our fears.

Sometimes what is at risk is too important; you feel like you can't experiment. The old adage of "Never gamble if you can't afford to lose" has some merit. Just remember that it can also be risky not to experiment. You may trip over an untested assumption or fail because you acted too conservatively. We often tend to overestimate the risk of a new idea and underestimate the risk of staying on the current path. There is no risk-free approach.

The Leader's Personal Experiments

For many of us, the biggest leadership challenge in fostering experimentation is our own inner sense that it's dumb to cherish the idea of making a mistake, let alone seek out opportunities to deliberately make mistakes. It's counterintuitive to believe in the value of errors and failed projects. However, if you want your organization to excel at innovation, you'll need to make that counterintuitive leap and manage this aspect of your culture.

This sense that it's counterintuitive to value the experiment regardless of the outcome often springs from all those childhood moments when mistakes were a source of shame. You probably didn't love those errors on your tests in school. Those experiences leave a lingering residue of feelings that makes it harder for you to see *experiment relentlessly* as a good idea.

The comfort of predictability is a second personal challenge leaders must confront to embrace the directive to *experiment relentlessly*. We love the illusion that we can control or at least predict outcomes in our organization. But human systems aren't controllable or even totally predictable. In focusing on predictability, you sacrifice experimentation and innovation. To fully support experimentation in your organization, let go of your need to predict and control.

Of course, there are the realities of project schedules and customer deadlines. Sometimes you will sacrifice innovation for on-time completion. Be sure that your culture doesn't fall so deeply into that pattern that it becomes the default. When your organization continually chooses predictability and control over innovation, long-term results will suffer. It's a balancing act.

C-level Teams

Experimentation can be more complex in the C-level than at other levels of the organization. You must strike a delicate balance. On one hand, if you aren't willing to acknowledge and learn from your mistakes in a publicly visible way, the Gorilla won't get the message. As the old saying goes, "You can't lead others somewhere you aren't willing to go." You must get comfortable being visible with your experimentation and learning. On the other hand, you don't want to appear not to know what to do. Most leaders seem so concerned about this risk that they aren't able to effectively model experimentation for their organizations. Find a balance point between these two risks.

Generational Differences

Today's workplace includes a wide range of ages, falling into several distinct generations. In most organizations, the two generations most prevalent in the workplace are the Gen Xers, who were born between approximately 1964 and 1980, and the Baby Boomers, who were born between approximately 1946 and 1964. Two other generations have fewer numbers in the workplace, but they are definitely participating. On the younger side, you have some Gen Y, who were born after 1980. On the older side, you have some members of the Silent Generation, who were born before 1946. Members of the Silent Generation and Baby Boomers (slightly less so) are reluctant to be wrong in front of the kids. These workers are in their forties and beyond. Many of them (OK, many of us) have children, or even grandchildren, who are the age of some of their coworkers. Especially for the Silent Generation, there is an expectation that parents are in charge and are presumed to be right. It doesn't feel natural for them to make mistakes in front of the younger employees. Gen X and Gen Y have come of age in a time when things are fast and temporary. You can start a business with an idea and abandon it just as easily. They are more comfortable with the notion that life is a series of experiments. This generational clash can make it harder for the Silent Generation and even the Boomers to fully embrace the directive to *experiment relentlessly*.

As I was exploring the idea of writing this book, I bumped up against my own Boomer mindset. I imagined spending months on end, slaving over my computer, before finally publishing the book and getting some reactions from readers. It was daunting. One day, I was discussing the project with one of my former graduate students, a Gen Xer. His advice was simple. "Write a piece of the book, and put it out as an e-book for free."

Wow, what a reframe! Soon after that suggestion, I released the first segment of this book as a short e-book. Hundreds of people downloaded it, and many forwarded it to their friends and colleagues. The feedback was very positive and almost instantaneous. My investment was small enough that it wouldn't have been a disaster if the e-book experiment had failed. Compare that fast turnaround experiment to the old model of traditional publishing that I had in my head. That's an example of the mindset difference in Boomers and Xers.

If you are a younger leader (Gen X or Gen Y) with Boomers or Silent Generation employees, remember that they didn't grow up with the concept of life as a series of experiments. They grew up with strong parental authority and a "Father Knows Best" mindset. This makes it even more important for you to talk about your own experiments—before they take place and after—and share what you are learning.

If you are a Boomer or Silent Generation leader, become aware of how you think about experiments, mistakes, and authority. When something doesn't turn out as planned, do you hear a punitive parent or teacher in your head, reminding you of all the times you've screwed up? If so, you need to unplug that mental tape. Figure out whose voice it is and let them know (in your own mind) that times have changed; experiments, and therefore "mistakes," are essential to success these days. Replace that punitive voice with a younger voice acknowledging and appreciating your willingness to try new things.

Multicultural Teams[5]

Not all cultures view mistakes the same way. Anglo American culture tends to be somewhat less formal than other cultures, so the loss of face associated with admitting a mistake is less crucial, although ego can still get in the way. Other cultures, such as Asian, consider the admission of error to be a loss of face that potentially threatens their sense of dignity and respect. To implement the directive to *experiment relentlessly* in a more inclusive way, you'll want to focus on the learning value of the experiments. In addition, find ways to lend additional credibility or respect to those at the heart of the learning. Make learning a high-status activity in your organization by recognizing and rewarding it.

People in different cultures also have different ways of coming to conclusions and understanding problems. Arab cultures rely more on intuition, whereas many African cultures use stories or metaphors and Anglo-American or Western European cultures tend to rely on empirical data and facts.

Your organization can benefit enormously by approaching learning and innovation with an eye toward all of these kinds of information. Think of quantitative facts, stories, and metaphors as different kinds of data. Don't dismiss a colleague's conclusion simply because he relies on a different kind of data than you do. Explore his sources of knowledge along with yours to see how the pieces fit together. If the different sources bring you to different conclusions, be explicit about your own approach, for example,

---

[5] *Please* remember that these are high-level, general statements about culture. All of us are affected by our cultural context, but we are also unique individuals. Use these generalizations to increase your sensitivity and awareness and provide a framework for understanding your team members, but *not* to stereotype groups or individuals.

"I'm going on my gut feeling here." Ask about his preferences, for example, "It seems like you're more comfortable explaining this through a metaphor. Is that right?" Acknowledging your different ways of knowing will help each of you listen to the other's perspective more fully. Then you can look for the synthesis of your viewpoints or an explanation of the disparity.

We've noted that to get your culture to embrace experimentation, it's important to deal with problems directly. However, in many cultures like Central European, Asian, Arab, and Native American, there is a preference for more implicit or ambiguous language rather than explicit statements. The Anglo American and Western European tendency to put your cards on the table may not be effective outside those cultures. You can still handle the problem rather than letting it fester; just be thoughtful about how you conduct the conversation. Choose language that is less pointed or direct, leaving more room for dialogue.

The Bottom Line

Your attitude toward experiments, both the successes and the failures, should tell employees that an experiment, even if it fails, isn't a "career limiting move;" it's an opportunity to learn. If you can manage your culture so that employees *experiment relentlessly* you'll have an organization that has the capacity to stay ahead of the competition and that can execute on its strategy.

Action Plan:

Experiment Relentlessly

- When a decision isn't producing the desired results, try something else.
- Acknowledge your mistakes; be open about what you learned from them.
- Seek out opportunities to experiment with doing things differently; recognize the learning opportunities inherent in the change.
- Build learning into your business processes.
- Deal directly with things that don't work; don't bitch and run.

CHAPTER 7

INTEGRATE RADICALLY

The gorillas were Fossey's most important stakeholder. The brilliance of her work lies in her ability to integrate radically with them. Her first sighting of the gorillas was at a distance, the gorillas watching the humans with an equal curiosity. Years later, Fossey had thoroughly habituated the gorillas to her presence. Some of them had begun to treat her almost as a member of the group. One day, Peanuts, a young male, approached Fossey and sat down beside her. After Fossey extended her hand on the ground, Peanuts "stood up and extended his hand to touch his fingers against my own for a brief instant." (p. 141)

Gorillas in the Mist

Can you cross a chasm as wide as the gap between species to get that close to your most important stakeholder? If not, you may be behind the times. "The medieval practice of putting a moat around the castle to protect its integrity from invasion is useless for our times," declared Stephen Zades and Jane Stephens in *Mad Dogs, Dreamers, and Sages.* Hence the directive to *integrate radically.*

This is more than just stakeholder engagement. I coined the term "outerprise" to refer to your enterprise radically integrated with all its critical stakeholders. The outerprise invites your stakeholders into your organization, integrates them into your team, and enables them to have a real impact on your business. In an outerprise, the Gorilla fully embraces key stakeholders.

Mixing metaphors for a moment, your organization is a small part of a much larger web, like a spider's web. Your web includes all of your organization's stakeholders. When you touch any part of the web, every part moves. Being an outerprise puts your organization in touch with your web. Being in touch enables you to connect more readily to your customers' needs, find new cost savings from partnerships, and be more agile in a rapidly changing environment.

Who are the critical stakeholders? Any individual or group with a stake in your organization, such as customers, suppliers, partners, end users, employees, investors and shareholders, the community, or even competitors. Their stake could be economic (investors) or more personal (employees). The stake is greater for some than for others. Some stakes are easy to understand; others are more challenging. Determining which stakeholders are most critical to your success and developing relationships with them is the core task in becoming an outerprise.

If you've ever been a hospital patient or had a loved one who was, you may have experienced a system whose processes were not designed with the customer (you) in mind. In some hospitals, everything from the way medications are delivered to the way invoicing is handled has been designed for staff and physician ease of use, not patient friendliness. The patient often feels almost as if she is an unwelcome intrusion into the hospital's business! On the other hand, my mother's recent experience in a small doctor-owned hospital was quite different. The staff members were competent, considerate, and respectful. Everything seemed to have been designed with the patient's overall comfort and healing in mind. This is hospital care the way it should be, with the customer as the central concern.

You want to integrate your critical stakeholders with your business. They are your life blood. Think of your business as an ecosystem. Remove the plants and animals from the human ecosystem, and we humans die.

Without your stakeholders, the fate of your business is much the same. But you're aiming for much more than survival. In the best case, each party's presence and involvement benefits the other in some meaningful way. That's what you want for your organization and its stakeholders. Understanding which stakeholders can make a difference in your organization's performance is critical.

Engaging your stakeholders and integrating them into your business can be perceived as a complex, even messy, undertaking. It doesn't have to be. Stakeholder engagement is simply about creating conversations in a way that leads to true collaboration. This can be done in a managed and structured manner, which removes much of the messiness and produces dramatic results for your business.

Let's look at an example where stakeholder involvement can have a huge impact. The typical approach to understanding customers is for the sales force or customer support to gather feedback regarding what customers want, need, like, and don't like. In addition, some companies host annual meetings to help them understand customers and receive input. These events are usually designed to provide information to customers and to make them feel valued. This is all well and good, but it stops dramatically short of tapping into the real strategic value that customers can provide.

If your culture has fully embraced the need to *integrate radically*, the scenario might be different. What if your customers got together with your executive team—not in a carefully scripted and staged event—but in a rich, juicy conversation, to explore possible directions for a new product? Obviously, this type of an exchange must be well-planned and executed—but consider the possible outcomes. Creating a genuine, open dialogue with your customers can provide valuable new insights for developing new strategies and innovative products and processes.

There are two major benefits to this type of open dialogue. You get an abundance of collective brainpower working on your success. Plus, your customers feel included and excited about what you are doing. The outcome is a win-win for your business, your customers, and as a result, all of your critical stakeholders.

The Mindset That Blocks the Outerprise

If the advantages of the outerprise are so clear, why haven't organizations moved in that direction more quickly? We know that in today's world everything is connected to everything, and yet we are still putting a moat around the castle. While our beliefs may not be as medieval as the castle moat, many of our ideas about organizations are relics from the industrial age when mass production and efficiency were the keys to success. Three archaic beliefs are likely to keep your culture stuck in its old patterns.

Scarcity: In the industrial age, the most important resources were physical, specifically land, machinery, and raw materials. In the age of ideas, physical resources have given way to mental resources, specifically concepts, ideas, and innovations. It's easy to see this if you simply think about the difference between a steel mill and a software company. The shift from physical to mental resources requires a new mindset. In the realm of physical resources, any given resource is limited in quantity. When you use some up, others can't have it. This breeds a scarcity mindset.

In the realm of ideas, if someone uses your idea, it often makes the idea more valuable. The Internet wasn't very exciting until companies like Google and eBay created content and tools. Granted, it's still possible for someone to steal your idea and take the value with her, hence the rise of intellectual property rights as a legal issue. However, for many ideas, the value goes up as the idea mingles with other ideas and other people use it creatively.

My generation, the Baby Boomers, grew up in the industrial age with parents whose roots were in the Great Depression and whose careers were mostly spent in old industries, such as automotive, petrochemical, and steel. It remains to be seen whether we will shed the scarcity mindset that came with that package or leave that task to Gen X and Gen Y, who grew up on the Web. Without that shift, it's tough to get your arms around the outerprise. If scarcity dominates your worldview, it makes sense to closely guard what is yours rather than looking for opportunities for collaboration and integration. In the world of ideas, operating from the mindset of abundance will produce more innovation and opportunities than a scarcity mindset can conceive or create.

Command and control: It's hard to get on board with the outerprise in a world of command and control. Again, in the Industrial Age, command and control management may have made sense. Efficiency and mass production were key success factors. Creativity in many jobs would have simply messed up the process. An assembly line works best when it functions in pretty much the same way today as it did yesterday. If you are going to become an outerprise, however, you'll have to give up the illusion of control. Human systems are complex adaptive systems. As such, they aren't very amenable to control; control is an illusion. Your external stakeholders certainly can't be controlled, so that mindset will have to fall by the wayside if your organization is to *integrate radically*.

We're not going to talk at length about complexity science, but let's take a very brief detour to understand how the command and control mindset needs to change. Organizations are complex in that they are diverse and made up of multiple interconnected elements. They're adaptive in that they have the capacity to change and learn from experience. This combination of qualities means they can be influenced but not controlled. If you've raised children, you understand what this means! For your organization to *integrate radically*, you'll need to accept this aspect of organizational life. You can influence your stakeholders, but you can't control them.

Dualism: The classic dualistic thinking that is so prevalent in Western society also gets in the way of the outerprise. Thanks to the separation of subject and object decreed by the scientific revolution, most of us think in terms of either/or. Although scientists now realize that observer and observed are two aspects of the same reality, this either/or mindset endures. In this mindset, your stakeholders can't be both separate from your organization (which of course they are) and a part of it (which they must be). So as long as this dualistic thinking dominates your organization's culture, the outerprise will likely remain out of reach.

Not all ethnic cultures have dualistic thinking as the dominant mode, so if your workforce is diverse and has a culture that supports the expression of alternative ways of thinking, you'll have an easier time breaking these barriers down. This is one reason that the cultural directive to *include respectfully* (Chapter 4) is so essential. The ability to hold multiple perspectives at the same time fosters creativity and innovation; the dualistic mindset often constrains our thinking unnecessarily.

Know Your Stakeholders

To make the outerprise real, you must understand your stakeholders. You can probably list them easily—employees, customers, suppliers, shareholders, your community, and others. You'll need to go well beyond that. Identifying key members of each group by name, for example, specific customers, is a good starting point. Who are these people? What do they need and want from your organization? Think beyond products. How would they like to do business with you? Consider your stakeholders as individual human beings with individual needs and wants, not just as a set of statistics. Put yourself mentally into their shoes and look at your business. When you are making a decision or planning a change, ask how the decision will impact your customer's customer or your supplier's supplier. Better yet, get them in the room and talk to them. We'll talk more about that in the next section.

Think in webs, not chains. When you think in terms of a chain, you see linear connections between your organization and its customers and suppliers. When you think in terms of a web, you can more easily envision that each part of the system affects and is affected by many other parts. You can consider the whole system of which your organization is a part. When your Gorilla is in the habit of seeing the interconnections among all of your stakeholders, your organization will be smarter, more agile, and more responsive.

This systems view of your organization's ecosystem can seem complex and sometimes overwhelming. Don't abandon it as a way of thinking. Complement this ecosystems view with a more simplified view. Some organizations accomplish this by declaring one stakeholder group to be the central focus. Southwest Airlines comes to mind, since I'm writing this on board one of their jets, headed to Dallas. For many years, Southwest Airlines has held the philosophy that if you treat your employees well, then meeting the needs of customers, shareholders, and other stakeholders will follow. That is not to say that their business processes are designed without regard to customer needs, simply that they believe that employee needs are the most important driver of success. They have been remarkably successful with that approach in a very turbulent industry. The clarity and simplicity of having a stakeholder group whose needs are presumed to take precedence over others can streamline decision-making and provide a base of stability in an atmosphere of constant change.

Arenas of Integration

Three arenas of your organization must be integrated with your stakeholders in the outerprise.

Information and Ideas: The first thing that needs to be integrated across your outerprise is the flow of ideas and information. The information that generally flows into and out of the enterprise is pretty sterile and carefully scripted A report on customer buying patterns, a carefully worded presentation about your strategy—these are fairly lifeless forms of information. Very little creativity is exchanged as this information moves across the boundary. That's not to say you should stop doing these things; rather that you should expand beyond these sterile representations of ideas and move into the messier terrain of genuine creative exchange.

A Fortune 500 technology company was suffering from supply chain inefficiencies. It took too much time to get a product from design to manufacture, and inventory turns were too long. Tom, the vice president of supply management, had pushed his team to make efficiency improvements for two years. They had made some good incremental gains. However, Tom believed that breakthrough gains were possible, and he set goals to drive that. He also believed in the outerprise.

To begin looking for the breakthrough gains, Tom created a supplier council consisting of his six largest suppliers. He convened the council for a facilitated dialogue each quarter. These were not the sales representatives or purchasing managers but senior executives from each company who came together to explore and address shared business issues. As you might expect, it took some work to build trust. Each quarter, Tom hosted dinner in a different fun setting to create an opportunity for social time outside the meetings. And, as the group's facilitator, building trust was my first priority. Once we had done that, having so much of the supply system in the room enabled incredibly creative solutions. Working with suppliers, Tom's team significantly reduced cycle time from design to manufacture and increased inventory turns. In addition, they implemented several other major cost-saving measures. The overall result was millions of dollars of savings. These goals were achieved not by pushing costs out to the suppliers, but by integrating the suppliers into business processes, pushing the exchange of ideas and information beyond sterile reports.

Get your stakeholders in the room and make a space for the exciting and sometimes messy work of creating something together. That will shift you from dealing with symbolic representations of the stakeholders to dealing with the real thing. It's like looking at the menu in a restaurant versus smelling and tasting the meal. Too often, companies confuse the meal with the menu. They settle for the menu because the meal might be too messy. This up close and personal approach builds trust throughout the outerprise.

Key Behavior:
Get up close and personal with your stakeholders.
Connect with your stakeholders, not just your data.

Processes and Metrics: Design your processes and metrics in cooperation with your stakeholders, with their needs as a key focus. To do this, you must know which of your stakeholders is most important, if not overall then for the particular process you are designing. You must look at the process as they see it.

Let's look at an example of how this might work in your organization. When you designed the problem escalation process for your service organization, what was uppermost in your mind? Did you focus primarily on the efficient use of your resources? Or did you invite customers into the design to tell you what they need from that process? Were the frontline services representatives in the room? Or did experts design the process using data about the representatives' work? Are your metrics primarily a reflection of efficiency? Or do they capture the quality of the customer's experience? Do you include metrics of employee satisfaction with the customer encounter? Or is that a separate matter for the human resources department?

Key Behavior:
Measure what matters to stakeholders.

Last month, my credit card company mistakenly recorded my card as stolen. After spending almost half an hour with the first-line customer support person trying to resolve the issue, we hit a roadblock. It was clear to me that we needed to escalate the problem to her supervisor. She was apparently rewarded for not passing issues to her supervisor. She did everything she could to keep me from escalating the issue. Essentially, she kept trying to talk me out of my problem instead of escalating it. The process and metrics were trapping her in behaviors that made me—the customer—very frustrated. Ultimately, I did get the problem escalated and resolved. Notably, while many organizations invite customers to complete a short survey after their support experience, this one didn't. The experience left me unhappy and they had no metrics to reflect that. The credit card company was not acting much like an outerprise.

To avoid this kind of situation, look at your organization from the stakeholders' point of view. Become a customer or supplier or shareholder, at least in your imagination. See what matters from that perspective, and find a way to measure it.

Key Behavior:
Design processes to include key stakeholders.

In recent years, many manufacturing organizations have found that they can reduce their product cost in a fairly simple way. The product design process is being modified to include supplier involvement earlier and earlier in the design cycle. As the process becomes more stakeholder aware, product design includes more supplier expertise. The final design is often more innovative as well as less expensive to produce.

Relationships: A transaction isn't a relationship. You know that. However, the culture and the systems and processes that reflect the culture may relate to the customer only in terms of transactions, even while the company has created a strategy to develop customer intimacy or relationship-based selling. If the Gorilla still deals in transactions, it will be a long, hard road to customer intimacy.

Consider the scenario of a large consumer electronics company known for its ability to compete on price. In the 1990s, predictably, the company took its support center offshore to reduce its support costs. Since the company focused on low cost, they failed to ensure that the call center staff spoke clear and fluent English or that they had good troubleshooting skills. Customers grew increasingly frustrated. Market share began shrinking. The company soon shifted its strategy to building relationships with customers. However, the culture still supported the old habits. Cost cutting was the top priority. Even though metrics were changed, the lack of explicit focus on shifting the culture caused the company to lose valuable time, and thus more market share, in the shift. The company ultimately rounded that corner, but it took much longer than it should have. Because they were managing products, customers, and finances—but not culture—they lost ground with their customers.

Of course, it's not only your customers with whom you need to build strong relationships. Your employees, suppliers, community, and other stakeholders are equally critical to your success. None of them wants to be just a transaction. If you think in terms of transactions or output only, your outerprise will not be as fully integrated as it might be. These relationships are the fabric of the web we discussed at the beginning of this chapter. To feel the vibrations in the web and respond quickly, these relationships must consist of more than transactions. Your culture needs to value relationships all across the outerprise. When you do, trust grows in your web.

Key Behavior:
Think and act in terms of relationships, not transactions.

Let's look at an example in the sales arena. For many sales organizations, getting a deal with Wal-Mart is the holy grail—highly prized, often sought, rarely obtained. It does not come easily to any vendor regardless of the products the vendor sells. In the typical sales environment of immediate results and focus on this quarter's revenue, winning a Wal-Mart contract can seem an insurmountable challenge.

After a three-year sales effort, one sales team was awarded a pilot order, potentially leading to millions of dollars of revenue. Raj, the sales vice president, commended the team on having persisted, despite the sales organization's culture not supporting this sort of long-term relationship-building effort. Raj knew it was more than determined selling. This sales team went against the culture. They helped shift their region from an enterprise to an outerprise by their slow and steady relationship work with one potential customer.

The Outerprise Within

So far, we've been talking about moving from being an enterprise to being an outerprise at the company level. You may be thinking, "How am I supposed to break down the barriers between my company and others when I can't even break down the silos within my organization?" If that's your situation, take heart. The same principles that help your organization *integrate radically* will help you break down your silos. In fact, breaking down your internal silos can be a great warm-up to creating an outerprise. You'll need to shift your organization's mindset (and your own) in the same way: escaping the scarcity, command and control, and either/or mindsets of the industrial age.

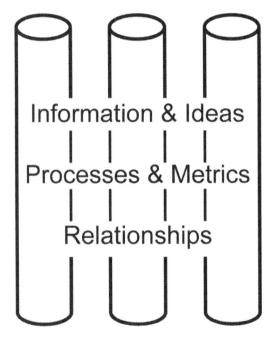

Information & Ideas
Processes & Metrics
Relationships

Marketing   Engineering   Production

The linkages are the same: ideas and information, processes and metrics, and relationships. In addition to the challenges mentioned previously, the expectation that it is someone else's job to create the linkages is a significant barrier to this application of the outerprise. Marketing team members wait for engineering to involve them in the product development process. Engineering team members wait for manufacturing to ask for their help in making products easier to manufacture. And on it goes. If you want to make the outerprise work within your organization instead of suffering in your silo, just do it. Create relationships. Ask other groups what they need from your group and how they would like to connect their processes to yours. This signals that silos aren't the way you operate.

Once you've built relationships that span boundaries, you'll find it's easier to create metrics that span organizational boundaries. For example, the cost to manufacture a product is influenced by design as well as by supply management and manufacturing processes. Similarly, the cycle time from prototype to volume manufacturing is a result of how engineering and manufacturing work together. If organizations share metrics, the culture supports looking outside the silos.

Multicultural Teams[6]

Two aspects of multiculturalism may affect your organization's approach to the outerprise.

Individualism/collectivism: Employees from an Anglo American culture tend toward a fairly competitive, individualistic approach. More than most cultures, they focus on individual achievement. This can make it challenging to create an outerprise mentality. The boundary spanning and collaboration that support the outerprise may feel more comfortable to people from other less individualistic cultures than it does to Anglo Americans. Leverage this diversity.

Low/high appreciation for context: The Anglo American culture is also what anthropologists refer to as a "low context" culture. While there are several aspects to the notion of high or low context, generally we can say that a low context culture understands events, people, or issues separately from the surrounding environment or context, rather than as an integrated element of the overall situation. In high context cultures, such as African and Latino, there is a tendency to rely more on context for understanding content. This high context orientation lends itself more readily to outerprise thinking. The outerprise can easily be seen as the context of the enterprise.

The Anglo American culture's low context orientation combined with its individualistic focus can make the outerprise mindset a significant mental stretch. If your Gorilla has learned to *include respectfully*, you'll find it easier to leverage your multicultural team.

The Bottom Line

When your organization integrates stakeholders across the outerprise, it will improve the quality of your strategic thinking. Perhaps the most fundamental shift is the ability to think in terms of the whole, not simply the parts.

---

[6]*Please* remember that these are high-level, general statements about culture. All of us are affected by our cultural context, but we are also unique individuals. Use these generalizations to increase your sensitivity and awareness and provide a framework for understanding your team members, but *not* to stereotype groups or individuals.

A shipping and logistics company was pushing for revenue growth to exceed 50 percent a year. In the early discussions, it became clear that as revenue grew, the sales districts would be divided to enable managers to stay close to the customers. Some district sales managers were focused only on the smaller geographical territory instead of the large opportunity that rapid growth was creating. Fortunately, Susan and her executive team were working hard to create an outerprise mindset both inside and outside the company. As they expanded the discussion to include conversations with partners and suppliers, the district managers shifted their thinking from their territory to the entire company. Through these stakeholder conversations, the lens shifted from parts to the whole.

This example also illustrates another change in strategic thinking: the shift from talking about stakeholders to integrating stakeholders into the process.

As you develop your strategy, it becomes natural to consider not only your customer but also your customer's customers and not only your supplier but your supplier's suppliers. This enhances your awareness of signals anywhere in your web. And it signals to your organization that the outerprise is real.

When you *integrate radically*, your company will be more in tune with the business environment. It will become more agile and less likely to be surprised by shifts in the external system. The likelihood that you'll prosper in the turbulence of the twenty-first century will increase dramatically when you manage this aspect of your culture effectively.

Action Plan:

Integrate Radically

- Get up close and personal with your stakeholders. Connect with your stakeholders, not just your data.
- Measure what matters to stakeholders
- Design processes to include key stakeholders.
- Think in terms of relationships, not transactions.

CHAPTER 8

CONNECT, REALLY

After a couple of what might be called "starter marriages," gorillas often mate for life. Rafiki and Coco were just such a pair. Rafiki was the silverback male and Coco, an elderly female. While the group was spread out feeding, Rafiki realized that Coco wasn't nearby and began to call out to her. She paused in her wanderings and began to head toward the sound. Rafiki sat down and waited. Coco climbed slowly toward the group. Once she could see Rafiki, they exchanged greeting vocalizations until she reached his side. Then, "they looked directly into each other's face and embraced."

Gorillas in the Mist

Now that's connection! No Blackberry or cell phone, just a heart-to-heart connection.

It's currently popular to refer to employees as "human capital" or "human assets." So much the pity! While those terms are meant to convey the importance of the "human assets" to the business, they make us less human and more like other inanimate assets. If you and your employees *connect, really*, you will all fully engage as human beings, not human assets. You connect with each other in genuine ways that have real value to the organization.

The shift to an economy based more on concepts and conversations than on land and capital demands a new level of personal engagement. If your ability to innovate and the quality of concepts you generate governs your organization's success, then anything less than genuine connection hinders your success. If your employees don't *connect, really*, your culture will fail to manage products and customers in innovative ways.

"Connect" probably doesn't mean what you think it does. It's not about how responsive you are to Blackberry messages, how many hours your work, or how many meetings you attend. It's about showing up fully human, connected to your own experience, and present with those you are working with moment to moment. It's about generating highly productive conversations by bringing all of who you are to your work.

Building genuine connections with others is an essential element of building trust. Many leaders acknowledge that it's hard to do. It's much easier not to reveal who you are and what really is important to you. When others have that knowledge, you become vulnerable. Because we don't want to be hurt, we don't bring all of who we are to work. This allows us to have the illusion of invulnerability. It also robs the organization of energy and blocks the development of trust.

As the new CEO, Mario had been hired to reinvent the company. He had been CEO of three successful companies before accepting this job and intended this to be the last company he built. Mario took the job knowing that a complete turnaround was required. Most of the senior team had to be replaced.

Mario worked hard to build a strong team and a culture based on trust. He and his new senior team spent time together off site each quarter, learning about each other and strategizing about the company's future. These sessions were intense as the team members built relationships and learned to trust each other. Mario's communication was clear and direct—everyone knew where they stood with him. If he didn't like an idea, he would say so in no uncertain terms. When someone rose to a challenge, Mario's praise was equally clear and direct.

It sounds like a great success story so far, and it was for about a year. The initial phases of the team's development went well, but they stalled out short of being a truly high-performing team. Why?

Mario had a temper. When he got frustrated with a stalled discussion in the senior team, he would pound his fist and declare the outcome. You've probably been in meetings like that. It's understandable that Mario got frustrated. He needed to learn to use the frustration to move the discussion forward in a positive way instead of letting his frustration control him. Without that, the quality of his connection with his team was compromised. Trust was eroded.

The Challenge: Self-awareness

The challenge for Mario was that he wasn't really in touch with his own experience; he wasn't aware of his frustration until it hit the boiling point. He was known for getting angry and then apologizing later. He knew that, even with the apology, his temper outbursts undermined trust in the organization. He tried managing his behavior,—controlling himself. It didn't work very well. Mario needed to tackle the problem upstream from the behavior. He needed to be more in touch with his own experience so he could feel the frustration before it hit the boiling point. That would have allowed him to use the frustration to help the team. He might have said calmly, "I'm starting to get frustrated with this discussion. It seems like we're going over the same ground again and again." This would have given the team a chance to pause and get back on track. It would have prevented the trust issues that Mario's temper outbursts created. But that required a level of self-awareness that Mario didn't have yet.

Self-awareness ⟷ Connections ⟷ Trust

Pat, vice president of sales in a consumer products company, had learned to use his self-awareness to bring more of himself to his job and be more effective. Anil, the vice president of marketing, had asked Pat to join him for a brainstorming session with their creative agency. Pat's son was having a serious health problem, and Pat's concerns about it were distracting him. As the meeting got underway, Anil wondered why Pat was quiet and withdrawn. Meanwhile, Pat was trying to get engaged and was aware that he was distracted.

After a few minutes, Pat finally spoke up, "My son has an important doctor's appointment later today and I'm having a hard time putting my concerns aside. Sorry about that." He sighed, then said, "Okay, let's get on with our work." After that, he was fully engaged. Pat didn't need to go into a lot of personal detail or make an emotional scene; he simply needed to bring that part of himself into the meeting.

We imagine that our distractions—family challenges, emotions, pressing problems—will get in the way of our work. However, what really gets in the way is our effort to compartmentalize our minds and leave our distractions outside. When we block out a piece of our experience, it takes away a part of our mind. Because the brain is more like a network than a filing cabinet, our awareness can't be easily partitioned off into self-contained boxes. When Pat tried to shelve the box labeled "concern about my son's health," he wasn't able to fully participate. When he opened that box and put it on the table, he was able to turn his attention fully to the task at hand.

Recently, I was meeting with the executive director of a nonprofit organization. She had been a client of mine several years before, but we hadn't been in touch recently. When we met, we had only an hour to spend together and she needed my advice about a significant issue facing her organization. First, we needed to reconnect across the time gap since we had last talked. That took about half an hour. When we delved into her issue, it was easy to reach a shared understanding of the problem and create several good options for solutions. The ease and speed with which we were able to do that was a direct result of the quality of our presence and engagement with each other. If we had gotten right down to business, that level of insight and creativity might not have been achieved.

Being truly connected as a human being enables useful ideas and insights because it develops trust and shared understanding. That trust also pays off in speed of execution. Teams that trust each other can make decisions more quickly. It makes it less likely that your culture will have a C.Y.A. mentality and more likely that members of your organization will be willing to *experiment relentlessly*. All of these things lead to more innovation and superior execution in your organization.

The Conversation Called Work

If creating high-quality, genuine connections is so good for business, why aren't we in the habit of making these connections? We carry around a myth that can block our willingness to be truly engaged with another person. That is the myth that we are stronger, invulnerable somehow, when we don't reveal our weaknesses or mistakes. Because we believe this myth, we try to keep parts of ourselves hidden. In reality, when we are secure enough for self-disclosure, our greatest strength comes from our vulnerability, our humanness. Others more readily trust us. No, you don't need to share the details of your personal life with everyone at the office, but you do need to be visible and vulnerable as a whole human being. You've got to stop believing in the myth of invulnerability.

> **Key Behavior:**
> **Connect to others from where you really are.**

Our desire to be invulnerable blocks our connection to each other and undermines trust. We can generally sense, at some level, when someone is hiding behind a mask. We know we aren't seeing the whole picture, and we feel less safe and less trusting. By sharing the things that are most important to us and that we feel vulnerable about, we earn others' trust.

In the industrial age, the quality of our human connections at work wasn't critical to the business. Now it is. In the age of ideas, your success depends on the quality of conversation in your organization. You can't have top-notch conversations without genuine human connections. David Whyte, author of *The Heart Aroused: Poetry and the Preservation of the Soul in Corporate America*, has said that the reason we crack our car windows when we go into work is that we leave our soul in the car and we don't want it to suffocate. We need to bring all of ourselves—body, mind, soul, and heart—back together if we are to fully connect with others.

Let's go back to Mario and Pat, from the opening section of this chapter. Unlike Mario, Pat was in touch with his own experiences, allowing him to connect to the conversation with all of his attention, not by pushing aside other things but by being open about what was actually going on for him.

For most of us, especially at work, our attention is focused outside rather than inside. For the most part, that is as it should be. We're paid to do a job, not to sit around reflecting on our inner state. Yet if you are too out of touch with your own experience, you will end up in Mario's situation. You can't avoid the fact that your reactions and emotions play a part in your ability to participate in the conversation called work. If you are unaware of those feelings, they may take control of you, as Mario often experienced. If you are conscious of them, you can use them to improve the quality of your conversations and thus your team's performance.

Being more connected to your internal state will also allow you to use your intuition more effectively. The importance of intuition in making good business decisions is well-documented. Your ability to access your intuition and use it to your team's benefit is directly related to your ability to be fully present with your own experience and your willingness to take the risk of sharing it with your team.

> **Key Behavior:**
> **Listen to your intuition; use those insights to benefit your team.**

Your intuition won't necessarily show up as a blinding flash of insight or a brilliant idea. Sometimes, it's as simple as noticing that you are uneasy with a plan and don't know why. Unfortunately, you won't have access to all of your intuitive wisdom and insights unless you are willing to show up and be fully connected to your own experience.

Chandra had been CEO of a professional services firm for three years, during which time the firm's revenues had doubled. To continue to grow, he knew the firm had to change its business model. The executive team had worked hard to create the new model. For it to be successful, the company needed to achieve a dramatically higher level of operational efficiency to support a new way of delivering its products at the same time it continued to rapidly scale up volume. Not an easy challenge. As the team planned the implementation of the new model, they decided a different organizational structure would provide more focus on operational efficiency. The addition of a vice president of operations seemed like the right solution. There was a solid, logical case for it and the team was easily coming to consensus. So far, so good.

As the team was beginning to discuss the unique skill mix the new vice president of operations would need to be successful, Chandra broke in. "I know this seems like a simple decision, but I'm uneasy with it. I'm not sure why."

He suggested the team take a minute to try to shoot the idea down and see where the conversation went. After a few minutes of discussion, it became clear that having a separate vice president of operations would create some significant disconnects in the workflow. Chandra intuitively knew that something wasn't quite right with the plan. He used his intuition to stop his team from making a bad decision.

The team then went back to the drawing board and came up with a new structure that reallocated some responsibilities among the top team and provided a more integrated work flow. This structure didn't require an additional vice president. If Chandra had not been willing to speak up without logic or facts to back up his gut feeling, the team would have made the wrong decision.

Trust

Without a significant level of trust, team members may not be willing to share an unfounded gut feeling. Developing that trust needs to be an explicit priority of the team. It won't automatically happen as you work together longer. You need time to get to know each other at a different level than is possible in your day-to-day interactions. You need to talk to each other about who you really are and how you work.

At your quarterly off-site meeting, include time to talk about the team. Yes, I'm assuming your team takes a couple of days away from the office each quarter to look at strategic issues that get drowned out by the noise of day-to-day issues. If you don't, you need to. In addition to tackling one or two significant strategic questions about your business during the off-site, plan on spending time talking about yourselves.

Key Behavior:
Spend time with the team focusing on getting to know each other.

You may think you know each other pretty well. After working together for a while, you know about your colleagues' children, pets, and hobbies. Right? At a deeper level, you need to know how your colleagues view the world and how their minds work. This strengthens your relationships and builds trust within the team.

At the first quarterly off-site meeting with the C-level team of a small technology company, the CEO asked each team member to tell one story from childhood that had left its mark on him. The CEO shared her own story first. Next, Jon, the vice president of development, described his experience building a radio with his dad when he was nine years old. As he told the story, the team could almost feel the bond forged between father and son, the joy of creating something together. It became clear not only why he had chosen a career in engineering, but also why he insisted on a highly collaborative approach to product design, and why he was so invested in mentoring young engineers. It was a small thing, not earth shaking, but Jon's story provided a window into the way he viewed the world.

As team members reveal more about themselves in this way, trust deepens. The ability to connect grows. The vice president of engineering and the vice president of marketing can connect as real people, not just as the occupants of those roles.

Connections ⟨⟩ Trust ⟨⟩ Results

Sharing personal histories in a focused way is one way to build trust. Additionally, you can use a style or personality profile to learn more about each other. Complete the Myers-Briggs Type Indicator (MBTI) or a similar instrument. Then discuss strengths and weaknesses as they relate to your job. This improves your ability to understand each other and communicate effectively. Several such instruments are available. Professional facilitation and guidance can help you use them to deepen genuine connections. Please be cautious. Don't use these profiles to label each other and be less authentic human beings! Use them to expand your understanding and deepen your connections.

Feedback

Building on that foundation of trust, ensure that team members give each other high-quality feedback. Use a 360 feedback instrument, and include a discussion of results in your quarterly off-site session. Rather than having high-level presentations, make this an opportunity for each team member to hear from his peers about examples and explanations of patterns noted in the 360 report. This builds trust and increases team members' confidence in their ability to give each other feedback.

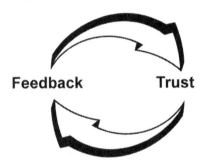

Feedback   **Trust**

Here's the catch about this feedback business. It takes a certain level of trust for team members to be willing to give honest feedback. One of the best ways to build trust is to give and receive honest feedback.

How do you break out of this Catch-22?

- Take small steps.
- Create opportunities for feedback in safe, one-on-one settings.
- Develop your own skills at giving honest feedback
- Give each member of your team feedback on a regular basis.
- Routinely ask for feedback; listen thoughtfully to what you hear.

As you begin to take bigger steps, for example, the 360 discussion described previously, have a facilitator present to help you. Otherwise, instead of building trust, you may either harm trust or reinforce the belief that it isn't safe to give honest feedback.

> **Key Behavior:**
> **Get good at giving feedback; do it often.**

Give your team a simple tool or model for providing routine feedback on a regular basis. You don't need a complex process, just a way of talking through what works and what doesn't. Virtually every executive team I've encountered needs to learn to give feedback with less discomfort and more impact. Managers often haven't developed this skill. It takes courage and self-awareness to provide useful feedback in the beginning, but after you've practiced a bit, it becomes natural and effortless.[7]

Regularly giving high-quality feedback reinforces the need for clear and direct communication. If you skirt around the edges of issues, it's harder for people to trust you. If you come out with both guns blazing, others will not want to expose their weaknesses or mistakes to you. Either way, the quality of connections among team members will degrade and your team's performance will suffer.

> **Key Behavior:**
> **Be clear and direct in your communication.**

C-level Teams

More than any other directive, *connect, really* demands leadership from the top. Letting go of the myth of invulnerability in favor of the reality of human connection takes courage and maturity. If the top team isn't able to model these behaviors, it's not realistic to expect that those at lower levels of the organization will have the courage to do so. This is both a challenge and an opportunity for the top team. The opportunity lies in the fact that when top leaders consistently demonstrate a willingness to really connect, others will feel the benefits of a more connected workforce. We like being human! Others in the organization are increasingly likely to connect more fully as they experience this connection from their leaders. The challenge is that you really do have to go first. You can't delegate it to human resources, and you can't just go through the motions. You must personally commit to leading with more authenticity and vulnerability to manage this aspect of culture.

Most likely, you haven't seen these behaviors demonstrated by your bosses and mentors very much during earlier phases of your career. The behaviors that allow you to *connect, really* aren't part of the Type A

---

[7] You'll find an easy-to-use feedback tool at www.FourthFactorOnline.com under Resources. Download it, and practice. Soon you'll be much more comfortable with this vital leadership skill.

personality or the Alpha profile that dominates most senior teams. It's ironic that top leaders need to model these behaviors first and yet they are often bred out of managers as they climb the corporate ladder.

Learning these new and often uncomfortable behaviors right in the middle of the pressure cooker of leading the company is a challenge. The day-to-day demands of the business keep you focused on financial performance, products, market needs, and other critical business elements. Finding the time and mental space to shift the way you connect to yourself and others at work takes a real commitment.

Multicultural Teams[8]

It can be a challenge to *connect, really* within your own culture, where the norms and assumptions about relationships and connections are familiar to you. In a multicultural environment, there are additional challenges. As you think about these issues, remember that being real and fully human is the foundation. The rest is fine-tuning.

Different cultures have different assumptions or starting points for relationships in the business context. The Anglo American culture tends to be task-focused with less importance placed on the business relationship. In other cultures, such as the Latino or African American culture, personal relationships and a strong foundation of trust are essential prerequisites to business. In the Eastern European culture, although personal relationships are highly valued, there is a tendency to be more reserved while the business relationship is developing. In Asian cultures, the emphasis may be on more structured relationships defined by social conventions. Be aware also that people from different cultures have different expectations about the physical distance between people. Be sensitive to cues that the other person feels you are too close or too distant for comfort.

The way different cultures express emotions varies widely, both among cultures and often within a given culture. In Asian and Native American cultures, restraint is valued above expression. In African and Arab cultures, open expression of emotions is typical, even in a business setting. In the Anglo American context, direct expression is valued, but there is an expectation that feelings will be expressed with attention to the impact. These examples highlight the complexity of this issue. To connect across cultures, you first need to be in touch with your feelings. That will allow you to make a conscious choice, based on your cultural sensitivity, about whether and how to express your feelings in a business setting.

---

[8] *Please* remember that these are high-level, general statements about culture. All of us are affected by our cultural context, but we are also unique individuals. Use these generalizations to increase your sensitivity and awareness and provide a framework for understanding your team members, but *not* to stereotype groups or individuals.

Each culture has a different approach to relationships. In each, the relationship matters; it just develops in a different way. Your ability to connect with your own experience will help you be authentic as you learn to modify your behavior to be more culturally sensitive. You don't need to be something you aren't; you simply need to be aware of your own habits and assumptions and those of others so you can *connect, really*.

The Bottom Line

Nido Qubein had run several successful companies and was on several boards when the board of High Point University asked him to become president of the university. They wanted someone who could help the university grow and become a truly innovative institution. Qubein is known as a tough-minded, high-integrity leader who demands results—just the man for the job. In his first year, he made many exciting and positive changes. The university was growing; students and faculty felt excited. The momentum for success was building rapidly.

Then the campus cafeteria's rating was downgraded from A to B. Qubein took this situation seriously and immediately began to address the issues. Meanwhile, the students began to grumble on Facebook. Qubein was already a Facebook member so he could connect to the students in their domain. He joined the Facebook group that was upset about the cafeteria. His first posting explained what was being done and, more importantly, how he felt about it. Commenting on the online grumbling, Qubein said simply, "This hurts my feelings." This was not something his PR staff told him to say. It was straight from his heart. The tone of the Facebook conversation changed immediately. The students began talking with Qubein about his feelings and theirs, and most of the students began to be more positive. Not because Qubein talked them out of their position but because he showed up as a human being with real feelings.

By wearing his heart on his sleeve, Qubein got the dialogue back on track. By managing culture that way, he was able to manage his customers more effectively. If you are willing to be present and visible with all of your vulnerabilities, you too can develop trust and create powerful connections in your organization. These connections are fertile soil for the conversations and concepts that will make your organization more successful.

Action Plan:

Connect, Really

- Connect to others from where you really are.
- Listen to your intuition; use those insights to benefit your team.
- Spend time with the team focusing on getting to know each other.
- Get good at giving feedback; do it often.
- Be clear and direct in your communication.

THE DIRECTIVES AND KEY BEHAVIORS

Question Rigorously
- Say "I don't know."
- Practice merciless self-awareness; reflect often and uncomfortably.
- Expose your thinking.
- Balance telling and asking.
- Attack issues, not people.

Include Respectfully
- Consider all ideas on their merits, not who originated the idea.
- When unspoken beliefs collide, actively engage in open exploration and dialogue.
- Consciously use casual social time to strengthen relationships among all members of the organization.
- Look for differences of opinion eagerly; treat them as signs that there are many right answers.
- Bring the distribution of power into organizational conversations.

Commit Responsibly
- Hold each other accountable as peers. Don't let the boss get stuck with this job!
- Voice commitments out loud. Never let silence be your form of commitment.
- When the team makes a decision, each member of the team supports the decision both verbally and with actions.
- If you can see that it's likely you won't meet your commitment, give your team a heads-up as early as possible.
- Sacrifice your own personal results or those of your organization when it is necessary to achieve a company result.

Experiment Relentlessly
- When a decision isn't producing the desired results, try something else.
- Acknowledge your mistakes; be open about what you learned from them.
- Seek out opportunities to experiment with doing things differently; recognize the learning opportunities inherent in the change.
- Build learning into your business processes.
- Deal directly with things that don't work; don't bitch and run.

Integrate Radically
- Get up close and personal with your stakeholders. Connect with your stakeholders, not just your data.
- Measure what matters to stakeholders
- Design processes to include key stakeholders.
- Think in terms of relationships, not transactions.

Connect, Really
- Connect to others from where you really are.
- Listen to your intuition; use those insights to benefit your team.
- Spend time with the team focusing on getting to know each other.
- Get good at giving feedback; do it often.
- Be clear and direct in your communication.

PART THREE

CHANGE

In Part Two, we covered the key directives your Gorilla's Guide needs to have in order to support your success. These six directives form an integrated system that will allow your organization to be more effective. Unfortunately, you can't simply hand your Gorilla a copy of this book and say, "Read this and follow it." That's why we're devoting the next four chapters to the pragmatics of managing culture.

To make the recommendations in the next four chapters easy to follow, I've separated the information into distinct themes with one chapter devoted to each. However, it's really not that tidy. Everything that has to happen for you to tame the Gorilla is interconnected. *State the directives*, *be the message*, and *second nature the behaviors* all form a system for managing culture. The challenge in talking about a system is that everything is connected. Because we can't talk about everything at once, we have to divide the system into parts, even if the distinctions are somewhat artificial.

In Chapter 9, Before You Start, we'll cover some foundation elements that you'll need to have in place. Vision, values, and trust are essential to your ability to manage culture.

Chapter 10, State the Directives, deals with the need to make explicit statements about your expectations using official communication channels. These statements form a foundation and supporting framework for the other actions, but by themselves they are not enough to allow you to manage your culture.

In Chapter 11, Be the Message, we'll talk about how to use your personal leadership power to manage your culture. This is more subtle and also has more impact than the official channels.

Chapter 12, Second Nature the Behaviors, tackles the complex web of both formal and informal systems that shapes your culture. By consistently and pervasively supporting your directives in both the formal and informal systems, you can hardwire your culture to make your organization more successful.

CHAPTER 9

BEFORE YOU START

"Human beings must decide now whether or not the mountain gorilla will become a species discovered and extinct within the same century."

Dian Fossey's ground-breaking work with the mountain gorillas of the Virunga Mountains was driven by her vision, first to understand and then to protect this "gentle yet maligned non-human primate." After her first visit, she was filled with a "compelling need to return to Africa to launch a long-term study of the gorillas." Over time she shared this vision with colleagues, staff, students, and volunteers. Almost three decades after her death, the vision lives on.

Gorillas in the Mist

Whether you are the CEO or a leader elsewhere in the organization, four things must be in place before you can manage culture effectively:

- Vision
- Values
- Trust
- Your personal commitment

Without these elements, your ability to make the directives in Part Two an integral part of your organization's culture will be limited. You can change the policies and procedures and write about the new culture in your employee newsletter, but without vision, values, trust, and commitment, it's unlikely that the culture will really shift.

Vision

The hard work of managing culture needs a strong force to drive it—a compelling picture of the future. When General Robert Wood Johnson created the Johnson & Johnson Credo in 1943, it described his vision and aspirations for the company.

Such an image of the desired future is a magnet that pulls your organization forward. To have that magnetic pull, the vision must live in the heart of every member of the organization. This emotional engagement provides the driving force for change.

The Johnson & Johnson Credo was initially handed down from the top without involvement from others in the organization. This is often the first stage in creating shared vision. A founder, senior executive, or team crafts a vision for the organization. It's a good step, certainly better than not having a vision. And you'll need more to ensure that the vision becomes a force in employees' hearts; you need to get them engaged with the vision. This has two main aspects: connecting to employees' personal aspirations and engaging employees in building the vision.

The manner and extent to which you include these two aspects in the development of your organization's vision will depend on many factors, including your leadership style, your position, and the current culture.

Connecting to employees' personal aspirations: When the vision is simply handed down from the top, it usually carries the message of "Get inspired to do this, or go somewhere else." That may not be said in so many words, but it is usually implied to some degree. To get your vision into employee's hearts, you need to create ways for them to explore their own aspirations and vision and connect them to the organization's aspirations. When employees can see how their future and the organization's are intertwined, the organizational vision will have more emotional power. Without that, it's just *your* vision.

Engaging employees in building the vision: In a vision-building process, a core team often spends a week or more exploring, studying, brainstorming, and arguing to create a compelling vision statement. Then, too often, they expect thousands of people to feel the passion after a sizzling one-hour multimedia presentation. All of the emotional engagement and personal participation the core team experienced is missing.

The more actively everyone participates in the creation of the vision, the more fully they will embrace it with their hearts. At different stages of an organization's and a leader's development, this is possible to different degrees. As the leader and the organization both develop, employees can be more actively involved in creating the shared vision. This requires that they have an increasing capacity for reflection, self-direction, and learning. In short, it requires an increasing level of leadership throughout the organization, not just at the top. And it requires that top leaders continue to let go of the command and control mindset and embrace participatory leadership. Figure out where you and your organization currently are in your development, and consider ways you might move forward. In the next chapter, State the Directives, we'll talk more about ways to engage with your organization about the key directives for your culture.

Values

Your organization's values prescribe how you want to operate on a day-to-day basis. How you will treat each other, how decisions will be made, and how you regard your customers and suppliers—all of these emerge from your organization's values. You might think of values as the philosophy behind the directives in your Gorilla's Guide. When someone asks why a certain behavior matters, your values should help answer that question. For example, from Chapter 7, Include Respectfully, why is it so important to allow the distribution of power to be a legitimate part of organizational conversations? Your answer might be that your company values state that "We treat everyone fairly." This adds emotional weight to the directive.

In Part Two, I made the business case for adopting each of the directives. The values case for the directives is personal and philosophical. Values have intrinsic merit; they don't need to be justified by the results they produce. What do you believe about your organization and how it should operate? You believe in integrity, trust, teamwork, and accountability. Great—so does every other organization (or at least they say they do). What do those words really mean to you? A clear, simple statement of these foundational principles forges a link between your vision and your directives. Together, the vision and values provide the "why" that will support you in managing culture.

Trust

Leading change requires trust. You'll be asking members of your organization to trust you, trust the process, trust each other, and so forth. If you're building on a strong foundation of personal integrity, you're halfway there. But you're only half way. Many high-integrity leaders view trust as a personal or interpersonal issue. They believe that acting with integrity, being trustworthy, is enough. At the individual level, it is enough. However, your aim here is to build a culture where trust is a given, where the culture supports actions that build trust among employees and other stakeholders.

Given that, you may be wondering why trust isn't one of the key directives. That would be somewhat like making water one of the five major food groups. We can't survive without water; it's part of us and everything we eat. So, it's not a food group; it's part of everything. That's the way you want to think of trust in your organization.

The following is a summary of the key behaviors from the directives that are most essential to developing trust in your organization. Each of these behaviors was covered in the appropriate chapter in Part Two.

Trust Behaviors—Summary

Question Rigorously
- Say "I don't know."
- Expose your thinking.
- Attack issues, not people.

Include Respectfully
- When unspoken beliefs collide, make time for open exploration and dialogue.
- Consciously use casual social time to strengthen relationships among all members of the organization.
- Allow the distribution of power to be a legitimate part of organizational conversations.

Commit Responsibly
- Voice commitments out loud; never let silence be your form of commitment.
- If you see that it's likely you won't meet your commitment, give your team a heads-up as early as possible.

Experiment Relentlessly
- Acknowledge your mistakes; be open about what you learned from the mistake.
- Deal directly with things that don't work.

Integrate Radically
- Get up close and personal with your stakeholders.
- Think in terms of relationships, not transactions.

Connect, Really
- Connect to others from where you really are.
- Spend time with the team getting to know each other.
- Be clear and direct in your communication.

Personal Commitment

On a recent girls' night out, Catherine began talking about some serious challenges in her marriage. Her twenty-eight-year-old stepson was refusing to grow up, and his dad always seemed to put the young man's needs before his wife's needs. She felt neglected and angry. We listened and offered various bits of advice and support. After a while, I asked, "What are you willing to change in yourself to change the situation?"

The group suddenly became quiet. I wasn't implying that the situation was Catherine's fault, but perhaps she wasn't ready to focus her attention on the one thing over which she has the most control—herself. Insisting that others change while you remain unwilling to grow and change is not the leader's way. A leader looks at each challenging situation as an opportunity for her own growth and development.

Managing your organization's culture isn't a program that you can delegate to human resources or hire a consultant to do for you. You can only take your organization as far as you are willing to go. We saw this problem in the story of Mario in Chapter 8. When Mario encountered an issue that required him to deal with his own personal development, he refused to address it. The team couldn't develop beyond the capacity of its leader.

Bill O'Brien, CEO, Hanover Insurance, puts it this way. "When a company transforms itself, 90 percent of that transformation takes place inside the people and 10 percent in process change and reorganization." As a leader, you must be willing to reflect, learn, and grow. If you're asking your people to change but you expect that you will somehow not have to change, you're kidding yourself.

When you want to shift the behavior of a human system, one of the most powerful things you can do is change your own thoughts, feelings, and behaviors. In Chapter 3, we talked about the importance of reflection and merciless self-awareness. Quality reflection time and useful feedback are essential to your leadership journey. To successfully manage culture, you'll have to challenge yourself to continually learn and grow. You'll have to tackle the difficult and unpleasant parts of your personal leadership development. You'll need to be willing to look long and hard at my question to Catherine, "What are you willing to change in yourself to change this situation?"

When your change program falters or gets stuck, which it will, the first step toward getting back on track is to look inside yourself. How can I align myself more fully with our vision and values? What part of me is resisting the change? What part of me feels unsafe or uncertain in this process?

Having a clear and compelling vision, well thought-out values, and a strong personal commitment are the foundations for managing culture.

The Arduous Journey

Managing culture is not easy. The principles in this book are meant to make the process more straightforward and understandable, but that doesn't make it easy. It will demand time, energy, creativity, and other resources from leaders at all levels in the organization. And the effort won't be finished in a single quarter. All of these challenges suggest managing culture is a focus that needs to be championed from the top. Don't underestimate the patience and commitment required to be successful.

Regardless of your position in the organization, you can be a leader by managing culture. Remember this when you want to give up and wait until "they" solve the problem. And, remember that the scope of your impact will depend on your position in the organization.

Let's talk about why top-down change matters and then we'll look at the options available to those leaders who are not at the top.

O'Brien led a culture change that helped move his company from one of the lowest performers in its field to one of the highest. In 1978, almost ten years into the change program, O'Brien presented a refinement of his ideas to his senior team and was met with what O'Brien described as "a long, respectful silence." In reflecting on this part of the process, O'Brien described the gradual adoption of some of the ideas, followed by "another damn presentation" where the team finally coalesced around the idea. (See Sugarman's article in *Reflections*.) O'Brien's vision, patience, commitment, time, and leadership had paid off. If you set out to create a major change in your culture, you're in for an arduous journey.

Because organizational culture and change management were new ideas in the 1970s, O'Brien and his team were truly breaking new ground. O'Brien's collaboration with some of the most brilliant minds in this field, including Senge, Argyris, Bolman, and others, created the foundation for culture change work that many organizations are doing today. Because we have that foundation, your culture change project may accomplish in five years what O'Brien accomplished in twenty-five years. And in a small company, the time scale may be dramatically shorter, but culture change is still very demanding work. And five years is a very long time in a world driven by quarterly financial results and instant feedback. Without a powerful commitment from the top of the organization, an organization-wide culture change effort is doomed to fail.

If you're not a C-level executive, you may be feeling frustrated right now. You've made it through most of the book and now it may seem that I'm telling you that an effort to manage culture must be driven from the top. Don't give up yet. Instead, choose an appropriate scope of action. Everyone can choose to be a leader by managing culture.

Whether you manage an organization of 10 people or 10,000 people, you can use these ideas to strengthen your organization. Even if you only manage yourself, you can make a difference. Think of yourself as CEO of the piece of the business you manage; change the culture in that piece of the business. Of course, you'll have to be prepared for that feeling of swimming upstream. As you change, the differences in how you operate and how other parts of the business operate will intensify. Your ability to lead by example may influence others to try your ideas, but be prepared to be out of step with the organization. You may have to justify your new behavior to senior management or your peers. And you won't have all the tools at your disposal that a top executive might have, for example, changing the performance appraisal system or restructuring the entire business. But you can make a difference in your own realm. You can manage the culture in your part of the organization to increase your ability to manage your other critical success factors.

Action Plan:

Before You Start

- Create a clear and compelling vision of your culture.
- Identify the values that drive your vision.
- Evaluate your team's level of trust-supporting behaviors.
- Assess your willingness to embark on a personal leadership journey.

CHAPTER 10

STATE THE DIRECTIVES

The gorillas exchange vocalizations to establish each other's location and identity—a conversation of sorts. Fossey learned to mimic this greeting and participate in their "conversations." She used this to allay their fears as she approached through the brush and also to "hang out" with them. Fossey announced to them, in their terms, that she was one of them and meant no harm.

Gorillas in the Mist

Announce your intentions to your organization just as clearly as Fossey announced hers to the gorillas. Communicating your cultural directives is a vital step in aligning your culture with your strategy. That's Management 101 stuff, right? Yes, and it's an essential foundation that can't be ignored. Let's go beyond Management 101 to see what will make the Gorilla pay attention when you *state the directives*.

Remember from Chapter 8 that the Gorilla's Guide has three tracks: official messages, events, and interpretations. You must align all three tracks to manage the culture. Communicating your directives explicitly will align Track 1 (official messages). That's the easiest of the three tasks. It provides a crucial foundation for all of the work you'll do for Tracks 2 and 3 (events and interpretations).

Directives: The Bridge between Values and Action

The directives in this book differ from company values or a credo in two important ways. First, directives are action statements; they tell employees to do something. Values are usually nouns like "integrity" or "excellence." If you want action, use action words. The directives in this book are all about action. Second, the directives in your Gorilla's Guide reflect the day-to-day reality of life in your organization, not just your stated aspirations. Your company values or credo are important elements of Track 1 (official messages) of the Gorilla's Guide. But that's only a small part of what shapes your culture. Tracks 2 and 3 (events and interpretations) are completely created from the experiences of members of the organization.

For many organizations, values are simply a set of platitudes hanging on the lobby wall or printed on a coffee mug. They're not integrated with the way the company is run. They're not aligned with the long-term strategy. They're just nice statements.

That's not what you want. You want your organization's directives to support your strategy and drive a powerful, execution-focused culture. That's why you're reading this book. If your directives are aligned with strategy and integrated with business practices, they are a strategic asset. At a very fundamental level, they provide a core of stability amidst the constant change of today's business environment.

Getting Specific

Beyond the high-level statements of your directives, employees need to hear expectations translated into specific day-to-day behavior and decision-making. In addition to being told to *experiment relentlessly*, they need to hear "Try it. If it doesn't work, we'll change it" or "We have a team de-briefing after every win or loss. No one gets shot; we explore and learn together."

If you provide only the high-level directives, two unfortunate things will happen. First, you'll avoid a lot of conflict and disagreement. Great, you say? Not exactly. The reason there will be less conflict is that when you stick to the high level, there's not much to argue about. Whether it's *include respectfully* or collaborate, what's to fight about? The conflicts are an essential element of your team owning the directives. You need enough specificity and substance to enable constructive conflict and shared meaning.

Second, since you're basically ignoring the principles of how the Gorilla's Guide works, the Gorilla will feel free to ignore you. In Chapter 2, we talked about the way the Gorilla's Guide shapes behavior and is, in turn, shaped by behavior, making it self-reproducing. That means that you're competing for mindshare with real events and stories that have color, texture, emotion, sound, and sights. Principles like *include respectfully* won't do very well against a real experience. Real events are memorable and emotionally charged, so if you want to get mindshare, get specific.

Don't use general statements like "The customer comes first" without telling employees how to translate that message into action. Too many leaders fall into the common trap of thinking that employees can consistently translate directives into actions on their own. It's not that your employees aren't smart enough to do that—of course they are! The problem is that each person translates the directives differently. The directives are somewhat abstract, by design, but behaviors are concrete. It's your job as a leader to ensure that the translation from abstract directive to concrete behavior happens consistently.

At the end of Part Two, I provided a summary of key behaviors to support the six key directives. Adapt and expand that list to fit your organization. Change the language to match your style. Add behaviors that fit your environment. Make the list of key behaviors truly yours.

Engaging Employees

The best way to make the directives into concrete statements that will guide behavior is to make that translation in a way that blurs the line between Track 1 (official messages) and Track 3 (interpretations) of the Gorilla's Guide. A well-designed process for developing your organization's key behaviors will allow you to guide the way employees interpret the directives and behaviors that you expect.

Many years ago, I was the philosophy director for Tandem Computers. Yes, that was really my job title. I was responsible for ensuring that the values were more than pretty words on a poster. Each quarter, we held managers' forums in which teams of managers discussed the application of the values in challenging management dilemmas—not simple right versus wrong situations, but those sticky right versus right dilemmas. The debates were heated; there were no "right answers" to these problems. At the end of the day, the teams shared their solutions with Jim Treybig, the CEO, and there was more debate. By the time they left, the managers had gone a long way toward internalizing the values. In the process, they also had explored the translation of the values into day-to-day behavior and decisions.

The forums succeeded in part because there wasn't much traditional teaching or presentation involved. The managers had to go through their own process of interpreting the values in specific situations, and they had to do that in teams. Why? We wanted them to have to actively listen to different points of view and engage in discussions about those differences. We wanted to involve participants in the process of creating meaning around the values as they related to the managers' own behavior.

What can we learn from this example? First, by bumping up against a variety of opinions, the managers came to a deeper, more personal understanding of the Tandem values. They bought into the values and really came to own them in a personal way. They heard how their peers interpreted their actions. Second, engagement doesn't have to mean participation in the creation of the directives or behavior statements. It can take many forms.

Your choice of engagement style must reflect your own leadership style and other factors about how your organization operates. If your leadership style is more directive than participatory and your personality is a strong factor in the culture, a centralized process involving only your senior staff is more consistent with that style. Such a process can produce a strong, direct statement of expectations that accurately reflects how you run the organization. Be sure to get employees truly engaged in the process. Give managers and other employees a chance to roll up their sleeves and apply the directives in complicated, messy situations that accurately represent life in your organization. Applying the directives this way creates a level of engagement that you won't get by teaching the directives or telling employees what to do.

Engagement ⟷ **New attitudes and beliefs** ⟷ **New behaviors**

In the Tandem example, the managers were engaged in applying the Tandem values, not in creating them. Tandem was a large, global organization and Jim Treybig had a strong, authoritative leadership style. The values were not meant to change the culture; they were intended to reflect the existing culture and ensure the culture remained consistent as the organization grew. Those factors all contributed to the decision to work out the values primarily at the top. While there was broad input into the values statements, the engagement process described previously was designed to help managers internalize and use the Tandem values.

At Johnson & Johnson, many years after the credo was written as a statement of the intended Johnson & Johnson culture, the company held challenge sessions to allow managers to engage with the credo. In these sessions, managers were encouraged to discuss what was and wasn't working about the credo and any ideas they might have to update it to reflect the current business environment. In this way, managers were constantly participating in the re-creation of the credo as well as its application. By challenging the credo and their own use of it, they were actively engaged in the process.

If you decide to have challenge sessions, you may want to ask your human resources professional or an outside consultant to facilitate the discussions. Be sure employees don't just point the finger at others who don't live out the values. Instead, ask employees how they might change their own behavior to be more aligned with the values. Create opportunities for constructive conflicts about the values and directives and their application. Use these sessions to provide a clear path for employees to criticize the values and directives. Be willing to hear that "It's just words on a poster" or other complaints about the values and their use in the organization. Then open a dialogue about how to solve those problems.

Whether you use meetings, surveys, blogs, or some other format, you want managers and employees to wrestle actively with your directives and the specific behaviors so the experience changes their thinking. That takes them beyond buy-in and opens the door for changes in beliefs and behavior. In that way, you affect both Track 1 (official messages) and Track 3 (interpretations) of the Gorilla's Guide.

On the other end of the participation spectrum, young companies often have most of the company actively participating in the creation of the directives and their behavior definitions. At one tech start-up that I worked with, the founding team and executive staff developed their core values. They then asked the rest of the company (only about twelve other people at that time) to help translate those values into day-to-day guidelines for the company. During that process, some of the values were modified slightly.

It was an iterative process, enabling everyone in the company to better understand each other and their shared goals. These conversations, like those in a challenge session, are also powerful because of the first principle of the way the Gorilla's Guide operates: employees continually access it without even thinking about it. These conversations about the directives and behaviors become part of that set of collective stories and are then accessed when employees unconsciously look to the Gorilla's Guide to see what is expected of them.

A Caution

A cautionary note about engaging employees in this process. Wherever you are on the participation spectrum, don't pretend to be somewhere else. If you or others in the organization have already decided how your directives translate into behaviors, don't try to create the illusion of participation. It wastes time and undermines trust. The most fundamental task of managing culture is to be real and authentic. Remember, you can't fake out the Gorilla.

If the directives and behaviors have already been defined externally, consider modes of engagement that acknowledge the existing directives and expectations. The most important thing is the conversation. When we are genuinely connected and in conversation about things that matter, engagement happens. Effectively managing culture requires that level of connection, engagement, and conversation.[9]

Now that you have some behaviorally specific statements to support your directives, ensure those statements find their way into all of the educational and informational systems in your organization. Work with your human resources, training, and internal communications professionals to make that happen. Drive for consistency across all of the systems and tools. The level of specificity, style, and medium will vary. The core message should not vary.

The Gorilla Will Ignore You If ...

If you want to *state the directives* and have the Gorilla ignore it and go right on doing what it's been doing, remember these three rules:

Stick to platitudes and generalities like "collaborate" or "involve everyone." If you're not specific, the Gorilla will feel free to ignore you. When you get down to specific behaviors, there is more for the Gorilla to sink its teeth into and it's harder for it to ignore you.

---

[9] For more ideas about alternative strategies for engaging employees in this conversation, visit www.FourthFactorOnline.com under Resources.

Communicate your directives once, and assume everyone understands. That way, the Gorilla can go on about its business as if it never heard you—which, by the way, it really didn't. When expectations are repeated in different ways using different media for a variety of audiences on multiple occasions, the Gorilla has to pay attention.

Present your directives to employees in a carefully scripted talk. Without engagement, the Gorilla has license to ignore you, no matter how often you repeat the message or how specific it is. Telling and presenting are not engagement. When you make employees part of the process, it becomes almost impossible for the Gorilla to ignore you.

On the other hand, if you want to be sure that the Gorilla pays attention when you *State the Directives*:

- Get specific.
- Repeat key messages regularly.
- Engage employees.

The Bottom Line

As they say in Monopoly, "Do not pass go, do not collect $200" until you *State the Directives*. Yes, some aspects of this are basic good management, but if you don't provide this firm foundation of expectations, the rest of your efforts to manage culture are likely to falter. As you *State the Directives,* keep in mind how the Gorilla's Guide works so you can modify it effectively.

Now it's time to move beyond *State the Directives* and consider Tracks 2 and 3 of the Gorilla's Guide more thoroughly. It's not enough to have Track 1 (official messages) aligned with the strategy while you allow Track 2 (events) or Track 3 (interpretations) to be at odds with the strategy. If there is any inconsistency among the tracks of the Gorilla's Guide, the easiest track to ignore is Track 1. That's why so many strategic initiatives fail. The strategic plan may include elements of messaging to get Track 1 aligned with the strategy, but I have rarely seen a strategic plan that took seriously the task of lining up Tracks 2 and 3. So let's move on to *Be the Message* where we'll address that issue.

Action Plan:

State the Directives

- Ensure your directives are action-oriented.
- Create behaviorally specific statements in support of your directives.
- Engage with members of the organization about the application of your directives in their day-to-day work
- Communicate the directives and behaviors frequently and consistently.

CHAPTER 11

BE THE MESSAGE

Every day, Fossey lived the message that she was friend, not foe. She describes the result of being her message. "Peanuts, Group 8's youngest male, was feeding about fifteen feet away when he suddenly stopped and turned to stare directly at me. The expression in his eyes was unfathomable. Spellbound, I returned his gaze—a gaze that seemed to combine elements of inquiry and of acceptance. Peanuts ended this unforgettable moment by sighing deeply, and slowly resumed feeding. Jubilant, I returned to camp and cabled Dr. Leakey [Fossey's mentor] 'I've finally been accepted by a gorilla.'"

Gorillas in the Mist

Human to human, what does it mean to *Be the Message*? Mohandas Ghandi said, "Be the change you want to see in the world." As was so often the case for Ghandi, he was giving both spiritual and practical guidance in one compact morsel. If you want peace in the world, be peace. That goes beyond acting peacefully and asks us to fully embody peace with our whole being. I'm not going to go off into a discussion of world peace or the spiritual nature of being. But I do want to look briefly at what happens to the system when you truly embody a specific change because that's what I'm asking you to do here—to fully embody the key directives that you want to drive your culture.

How does that shift the system? It's like a dress rehearsal for the future. You show up totally in the desired future state and you get to see how others react. You learn what needs to be tuned to give coherence to that future state. Only now it's not totally in the future. It's here now; you are embodying it. Everyone in the system is getting a chance to experience her or his actions and see the impact in a new context because of the new way you are being in the system. This dress rehearsal for the future begins to create that future in the present.

Let's talk about how this all works in the Gorilla's Guide. By being the message, you can alter Track 2 (events) and Track 3 (interpretations) so they align with the official messages in Track 1. Four aspects of being the message are essential to this alignment:

- Self-awareness
- Feedback
- Trust
- Meaning-making

Each aspect plays a crucial part in being the message. While *State the Directives* was concerned mostly with official communications, *Be the Message* goes to the heart of your personal leadership.

Self-awareness

This is not a typical topic for most discussions of organizational culture, but without it, your ability to *be the message* is limited. Why? Because you're not perfect. You're going to do and say things that are not perfectly aligned with your directives. That's not the end of the world—we'll talk more about mistakes later. But it means you'll need to have enough self-awareness to be conscious of your actions, the impact on others, and the way others may interpret your actions. This awareness is your first tool in tuning your leadership.

I want to focus on your self-awareness in the context of the directives. Become aware of your behavior and beliefs in relationship to your directives and desired behaviors. You may be creating your organization's directives, or the directives may have been around long before you joined the organization. In either case, it's time for some soul-searching. Consider each of the directives and its associated behaviors. Imagine how it would be if your behavior was fully aligned with the directive. How would you operate on a day-to-day basis? This calls for some uncomfortable reflection and merciless self-awareness. The surface answers aren't enough.

Consider this example of *experiment relentlessly*. One of the key behaviors for that directive is "Deal directly with things that don't work." Imagine your organization has that directive and behavior expectation. Let's say you're the vice president of services. You're having difficulty with the vice president of development. No matter what you do, she doesn't give you a heads-up about changes early enough in the cycle. You're frustrated. Is it tempting to sit down with the sales vice president and spill your guts about what a pain the development VP is? How do you feel when you realize that you shouldn't have that conversation but instead should go to the development VP personally? What if you're the sales VP in this story? Are you going to tell the services VP that you're not willing to have that conversation because he needs to take it to the development VP? "Deal directly with things that don't work" includes some uncomfortable behaviors. These are the challenging personal moments when your leadership really matters. How aligned are you ready to be?

These are small moments, not big strategic decisions. But if you are going to *be the message*, these small moments matter—a lot. These small moments add up to Track 2 (events) of the Gorilla's Guide. They signal that you're serious about your stated directives, which gives you greater ability to manage the culture.

When I ask you to imagine how it would be if your behavior were fully aligned with the message, I'm asking you to reflect at the level of these small, private moments, not just the public events, and to be brutally honest with yourself about what you see. Otherwise, your self-awareness sits on a shaky foundation. Others will not do what you aren't willing to do first.

Part of the problem is that you may have spent years working in organizations where these key behaviors were not the norm. The culture in those other organizations has left its mark on you. According to the first principle of the Gorilla's Guide, that we access it without thinking, you unconsciously access all of that cumulative information constantly, and it shapes your behavior.

Being honest with yourself about whether you are following the directives in your current organization is the first step to self-awareness and alignment. Next, identify any gaps between your current behavior and that fully-aligned image. Don't let yourself off the hook because you see others who aren't fully aligned. Focus on yourself. Decide whether you are willing to work on areas that need improvement. Are you willing to be in learning mode in these areas? Are you motivated to seek out and listen to feedback about these gaps?

Feedback

The more power you have in the organization, the less likely it is that you're getting clear, useful feedback, which is essential to your learning. Whatever your role, develop sources of direct, honest feedback. Anonymous feedback can also be useful in this process. You need data about the impact your behavior has on others. While you may have lots of empathy, you can't get inside others' heads to see how your actions impact them unless they are willing to tell you. Only then can you learn whether your intentions and your impact match and see how others interpret your actions.

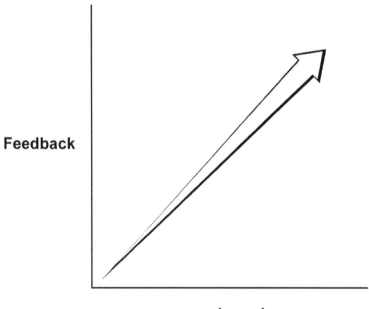

Feedback

Learning

The best way to get better feedback is to get everyone on your team engaged in actively exploring the alignment between the directives and team members' behavior. As a team, you can learn to observe your own actions and align them more closely to the directives. A good starting point is to have team members read this book and have a discussion about this section.

Talk with your team about why you personally want to continue to improve the alignment of your actions to the directives. This conversation needs to come as much from your heart as your head. It's as much a personal message as an organizational message. This is a place where you need to practice the *connect, really* directive. You must show up real and human with your vulnerabilities showing. Otherwise, the feedback and alignment process can be just another management fad. Learning to manage culture is a personal leadership journey. To get your team on board, you'll need to get personal about what this journey means to you. Take time for team members to talk about the challenges and opportunities of the changes and what it means to them personally. When your team is on board, then you're ready to work together on giving each other feedback.

The CEO of a large nonprofit organization and his team were having their quarterly planning retreat. The meeting was held in a lovely mountain retreat center, spacious and open with cozy, living room-style seating. As he often did, Hakim, the vice president of operations, pulled his chair back away from the group so he could stretch out his long legs. At six-foot-two, he was happy to have the room to get comfortable.

It had been a successful day. The team clarified an ambiguous strategy and reset priorities. But the vice president of marketing, Sabina, was clearly uncomfortable and she spoke up. "Hakim, I keep wondering why you're sitting a little apart from the group. It makes me feel like you're not part of the team."

After a brief, somewhat awkward silence, Hakim entered into a discussion with the team about this perception. Because of his long legs, Hakim often pulled his chair back at team meetings. He learned how his choices about seating were impacting the team, and they learned why he sat as he did. It was a small thing, but it started a more open exchange of feedback and perceptions than the team had shared before. This simple conversation helped move the team forward.

To improve the quality and quantity of feedback in your team, pay attention to four areas.

Assumptions that block feedback: Many successful managers and executives lack experience giving and receiving useful feedback. We think we know how our actions are perceived, mostly because we make the mistake of assuming that the person on the receiving end of our actions sees our actions the same way we do. We also assume others know how they are perceived, or worse, that they don't want to know. These assumptions get in the way of good feedback. You and your team will need to set these assumptions aside and open new channels of effective feedback. Developing your team's ability to exchange honest feedback will make a significant difference in your ability to *Be the Message* and in your team's performance.

Positive feedback: You might think that giving positive feedback would be easy, but surprisingly few managers, especially at the executive level, give positive feedback regularly. Managers often assume that others know what they are doing well. That may or may not be true in any given situation. Either way, what is true is that you can shape behavior very effectively by acknowledging and appreciating what is already working and building on strengths. Simply telling someone what she did well and the positive impact it had can be very powerful. By focusing attention on what works, you strengthen those patterns. As your team develops its alignment with the directives, be sure to acknowledge positive points of alignment whenever you see them.

Trust and openness: Many teams lack the trust and openness to make honest feedback a real option. Instead, team members often hold back their opinions or soft pedal the intensity of their ideas when giving critical feedback. Consider this situation. Kohana had been part of the marketing team for about three months when a friend told him that Roger, a more senior member of the team, felt Kohana was reacting defensively in team meetings. Kohana went to Roger and asked him directly how he could make a better contribution in team meetings. Roger replied that Kohana was doing fine. Kohana asked a couple of other questions to elicit useful feedback, but he finally left Roger's office, no more enlightened than when he arrived. It wasn't that Roger didn't have anything to say, but rather that he didn't feel comfortable saying it to Kohana. Roger had talked with human resources about it and muttered to his friend about it, but he wouldn't give Kohana the feedback directly. There simply wasn't enough trust.

Willingness to learn from mistakes: As you learn to *be the message*, don't expect perfection of yourself or others. Be willing to learn together from your mistakes. You may find that there is a gap between what you thought your actions conveyed and what others experienced. It's simply not possible for you to be 100 percent accurate in calibrating the impact of your actions in advance. That's why feedback is so important. It's also why you need to be accepting of mistakes, both your own and those of your team members. That doesn't mean that you ignore it when you miss the mark. You address it. If it's your mistake, you acknowledge it and apologize if necessary. If someone on your team has missed the mark, talk to her directly and thoughtfully about the issue. Creating a safe climate in your team enables all of you to learn from your mistakes.

Giving and receiving feedback is crucial to your ability to manage your organization's culture. As the second principle of Gorilla's Guide operation tells us, the Guide is constantly being updated. High-quality feedback helps ensure that those updates are continually getting closer to the target, not further away.

If your team members don't trust each other enough to give direct feedback, make building trust a top priority. Honestly assess your performance on the trust-building behaviors summarized in Chapter 9. You may need to begin with anonymous feedback, collected either online or by a third party. Ultimately, you need to be able to discuss these issues as a team.

If you are willing to pay attention to the alignment between the directives and your actions on a day-to-day basis, you can keep the directives from being another management fad. *Be the message*. Live it and breathe it every day.

Meaning-making

In addition to walking the talk, that is, living and breathing your directives daily, you have to talk the walk. If your directives and your actions are aligned, you'll have a great setup for this aspect of being the message. In Chapter 10, State the Directives, we talked about communicating what is expected of employees—the directives and the behaviors. You also need to communicate why you have taken a specific action in terms of the expectations inherent in the directives. Wrap the actions in an envelope of meaning; become a meaning maker in your organization.

Remember the Disney story? Walt Disney knew why he was chatting with the maintenance workers, but what if he hadn't explained? Perhaps that incident would have been stored in the maintenance supervisor's personal Gorilla's Guide as "proof that upper management doesn't understand how busy we are." After all, the head boss was taking several guys off duty just as the supervisor was trying to be sure the park was ready to open. Mr. Disney got a chance to edit the interpretation in the Gorilla's Guide before it got stored and before it hit the grapevine. He didn't make a long, prepared speech. Disney simply explained his own authentic reasons for what he had done.

As a leader, when you give a short, simple explanation of why you took a specific action, you shape Track 3 (interpretations) of the Gorilla's Guide recording. This is your chance to be a meaning maker in your organization, and that's a powerful role. Explaining the logic or rationale at the moment something happens or is announced is a particularly powerful leverage point because you are editing as the data is being stored, not trying to change something that is already squirreled away. The scope of your impact will vary depending on your role in the organization. If you are a senior executive, you have an opportunity to influence interpretations across the organization. If your influence and authority are more limited, you can still make a difference within your part of the organization.

When you set the Track 3 recording effectively, you maximize the positive impact of the third principle, that the Gorilla's Guide and behavior shape each other. Your explanation significantly enhances the positive impact of the events.

This explanation is not spin. When you spin something, you are trying to make it appear to be something it's not, to turn the proverbial sow's ear into a silk purse. This brief explanation of a decision is the opposite. It's often going to be off the cuff, not prepared remarks. It's more from your heart than from the PR folks. By providing a genuine and authentic explanation of how the messages you shared shaped your action, you offer an interpretative lens through which employees can understand what has happened. This guides your organization. If your action isn't congruent with your messages, no amount of explanation or spin will work. The Gorilla laughs at spin. If you can clearly communicate why an action was taken in a way that is genuinely linked to your directives, the Gorilla will listen.

The Bottom Line

Being the message is a daily discipline of leadership. It's how you shape your employees' experience of the organization. By constantly tuning your own alignment with your directives, you can manage the culture of your organization.

Action Plan:

Be the Message

- Increase your awareness of how your own behaviors align with your directives.
- Get feedback about the impact of your actions relative to your intentions.
- Give positive feedback about alignment with organizational directives whenever there is an opportunity.
- Provide short, simple explanations of how your actions and decisions align with your directives.

CHAPTER 12

SECOND NATURE THE BEHAVIORS

How do you get a group of people-shy gorillas to come out in the open so you can observe them? Make it too appealing to resist, not with goodies and treats, but by aligning with their natural curiosity. One cool damp morning, Fossey tried to climb a tree to get a better look at the gorillas. "I naturally assumed that the combined noises of panting, cursing, and branch-breaking made during the initial climbing attempts must have frightened the group on to the next mountain. I was amazed to look around and find that the entire group had returned and were sitting like front-row spectators at a sideshow.... That day's observation was a perfect example of how the gorillas' sense of curiosity could be utilized toward their habituation. Nearly all members of the group had totally exposed themselves, forgetting about hiding coyly behind foliage screens."

Gorillas in the Mist

If you create systems that naturally align behavior with the directives, members of your organization will forget about hiding from the change. The idea is to make alignment virtually inescapable. No matter what an employee does or where she turns, something is nudging her toward the expected behavior.

So much of culture is outside of our awareness. You and your employees often behave the way you do out of habit, in unconscious conformance with the culture. It takes repetition of the new behaviors over time to make a shift in the culture. Everyone needs to see evidence of the messages in action over and over.

It's a little like watching a mystery movie. You're not quite sure who is the good guy and who is the bad guy. Little snippets provide clues; then there is the scene where two people exchange a glance, and you understand what's going on. Without the earlier clues, it wouldn't have made sense; each glimpse seeded the idea. It's all about consistency and repetition.

Events and stories work the same way in the Gorilla's Guide. Each one builds on another as the pattern emerges. It's essential that you develop consistency across both formal and informal systems so there is a preponderance of stories that support the directives. The mutually reinforcing interaction between the Gorilla's Guide and behavior makes culture self-perpetuating. That's why it's so essential that your official and informal systems reflect the directives consistently.

The Org Chart

You can use official systems, for example, organizational structure, escalation processes, performance reviews, and compensation plans, to nudge the Gorilla toward new behaviors. For example, the organization's structure gives members of the organization messages about who really needs to be involved in what areas and how they should interact.

Remember the story in the introduction about my experience as a hardware product manager at Tandem? The separation of hardware and software all the way up to the CEO made my job much harder than it needed to be. The software product manager and I both made an extra effort to coordinate with each other, but the structure and culture blocked our path at every turn. We were competent, well-intentioned people working in a flawed structure.

Maybe there was a rational explanation for that structure. Still, organizational structure, like most of the official systems, is a reflection of the culture. The separation of hardware and software was consistent with Tandem's culture at that time. And that structure also helped to create and re-create that culture. Again, we're encountering the self-perpetuating nature of culture. That's where your leadership opportunity comes into play. Having thought through how your culture will support your strategy, you have the opportunity to change the official systems so they influence the culture the right way. Instead of letting the Gorilla create the organization chart without regard for your strategy, you can create the organization chart as part of managing the culture of your organization.

You may think it's absurd to talk about the Gorilla creating the organization chart. Before you dismiss the idea, think about all the unspoken assumptions—the so-called givens—that were at play the last time you restructured your organization. For example, perhaps in your organization "everyone knows" that product marketing has to be in engineering, not marketing, or that the U.S. sales region "must" be a separate organization from the rest of North American sales.

Most teams have a very hard time seeing all of the assumptions, beliefs, and givens that shape their organizational structure and other formal systems. If you can't see them, it's very hard to make choices about them. That means the Gorilla is probably making the choices for you. On the other hand, if you can challenge these givens, you may find new ways to align your structure with your strategy and thus get the culture to support the strategy more effectively.

Hiring

I've been talking mostly about organizational structure. It's a very visible and powerful manifestation of the culture. Let's look at another official system that exerts a pervasive influence on your culture—your hiring system. Hopefully you have a consistent process for ensuring that everyone you hire has the skills to be successful. If you're serious about managing your culture, you also need to ensure that everyone fits your culture. Assess cultural fit with the same level of structure and rigor as you assess skills.

The graphic illustrates the integration of culture fit and skills fit in your hiring process. If you aren't explicitly focused on hiring for culture fit, your process is probably designed to reject unskilled candidates but is less effective at filtering those who aren't a good culture fit. Strengthen your hiring process so you will hire only those who will be successful in your environment—those who are both a skills fit and a culture fit.[10]

---

[10] For specifics on how to hire for culture fit, go to www.FourthFactorOnline.com under Resources.

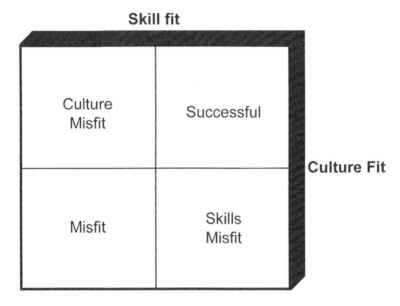

Bjorn had been CEO of the young biotech company for about six months. He had inherited a culture of fear and mistrust where accountability was a foreign concept. He replaced several members of the senior team. The new team was highly aligned in its intent to create a culture of trust and accountability. But the old culture still seemed to have a hold on the company. Bjorn found himself asking not only some of the more senior employees but also some recent hires to leave the organization because they weren't aligned with the new culture. It felt like a constant dance of two steps forward and one step back. They were making progress, but not quickly enough. Bjorn decided to redesign the hiring process to place equal emphasis on culture fit and skills. Then he taught managers how to assess culture fit. Six months later, Bjorn told me that everyone he had hired since the rollout of the new system fit the culture—no hiring mistakes! By managing culture proactively, Bjorn made it easier to manage the business successfully.

Just as you should hire for cultural fit, you also want to use your performance management system to reinforce your directives. If *experiment relentlessly* is one of your directives, the system should reward intelligent risk and learning by doing, not just successful experiments. If you want people to *connect, really* by exhibiting the key behavior of "Be clear and direct in your communication," design your performance management system to support managers in giving frequent, clear feedback.

Other Systems

You can apply this discussion about the Gorilla's role in shaping the organization's structure or the performance management system to any of the other official systems. Each official system is both a reflection of and a crucial influence on your culture.

All of these systems signal what the organization values and how things should be done. Working with the official systems is the easiest part; these systems are the most visible and changes can be made programmatically. That's crucial, but it's not effective by itself.

Too often, leaders seem to believe that they can manage culture by simply offering performance bonuses, setting goals, or having an employee communications campaign without the leaders changing how they actually behave. The sales vice president who put a new opportunity planning process in the field and required sales reps to use it is a classic example. When the vice president failed to use the opportunity plans in weekly team meetings or when making decisions, the system died on the vine. Why? Tracks 2 and 3 (actions and interpretations) are more powerful and influential than Track 1 (official messages). That means that you've got to have both your official and informal systems supporting the official messages.

Seven Habitats

While the official systems are visible examples of official power in your organization, informal systems are manifestations of the Gorilla's power. Consider these seven habitats of the highly elusive Gorilla:

- Cubicles, offices, and hallways
- Blogs
- Copier and printer rooms
- Social networking sites
- Cafés
- Instant messages
- Staff meetings

All of these are part of the invisible fabric of your organization. You can't control these systems like you can the official systems. But you can—and must—influence them.

There are many examples of what happens when there is too much tension or discord between informal systems (the Gorilla's power) and official systems. The opening story in this book of what happened to Fiorina at

Hewlett-Packard is a classic. You don't want to get caught in that sort of conflict. That's why you must align the informal systems as well as the official systems with your directives to signal what really matters.

For example, as part of your *integrate radically* directive, one of your key expectations might be "Build customers for life, not transactions." For your informal systems to support that message, ensure that you bring up the subject of customer satisfaction and relationships in meetings and conversations regularly. In your staff meeting, do you review the sales forecast, discuss new opportunities, and review wins and losses, but fail to make time to talk about customer satisfaction and relationship development? If you have a war room dedicated to closing new sales, how about a peace room dedicated to building customer relationships? These are examples of the ways you can get your informal systems to support your message. Don't miss out on opportunities to get Tracks 2 and 3 (events and interpretations) of the Gorilla's Guide aligned with Track 1 (official messages).

Remember, when Track 1 is out of sync with Tracks 2 and 3, the Gorilla is more likely to ignore Track 1 and act on Track 2 or 3. Track 1 is simply not as rich and compelling as Tracks 2 and 3. It's like an audio-only recording compared to a jazzy multimedia presentation. Which one gets more attention? Which one can more readily grip you emotionally? Which one will you remember? Tracks 2 and 3 are that compelling multimedia presentation, and that's what has impact.

It's the consistency of the message across both official and informal systems that shapes your culture. Build systems that support the behaviors you want reflected in the stories in your Gorilla's Guide. The systems will provide a structure that guides the members of your organization to behave in new ways. Over time, the self-reproducing aspect of culture will turn in favor of the new directives.

Earlier, we talked about Bjorn's system for ensuring that new hires fit the new culture. In addition to the official system, Bjorn made a crucial decision that helped ensure the support of the informal systems. He decided to be the interviewee in the demonstrations during the rollout of the new system. More importantly, he decided to play the part of himself being interviewed for his current CEO role. When the demonstration interviewer asked him the behaviorally specific interview questions, Bjorn told real stories from his own career experiences. The impact on Tracks 2 (events) and 3 (interpretations) of the Gorilla's Guide was huge. Managers talked about these personal stories that the CEO had shared for weeks. The official system (hiring) and the grapevine were aligned with the new directives.

Coaching

In Chapter 11, you learned how to *be the message*. Those ideas and tools enable you to be a model for others. You are using your own behavior to show others what you want. By providing feedback and coaching to help others align their behavior with the directives, you will magnify the impact of your modeling.

Acknowledge others' alignment: Look for opportunities to acknowledge and appreciate others whose behaviors are aligned with the directives. For example, what if, "Deal directly with things that don't work" is one of the expectations in your organization? When someone comes to you with a problem she is having with you, simply acknowledge that it's sometimes tempting to talk to others about such a problem and you appreciate that she had the courage to come directly to you. Tell her why that matters to you. This kind of informal, positive feedback supports the new behaviors and may create stories that circulate on the grapevine.

Once again, these are small moments, not big public events. The Gorilla's Guide needs to be full of these small moments when employees experience their own alignment with the directive and see that it makes a difference.

Be visible with your learning: Be transparent about your own challenges. For example, if your directives include *question rigorously* and you find it hard to say, "I don't know," then you can acknowledge that. For some people, it's easier to admit this with humor. For example, say, "Bet you thought I'd never admit this, but I don't know." The more you allow others to see your own learning process, the more they will be willing to learn from their own challenges.

These two techniques are a more subtle and less directive form of coaching than most leaders practice. You are using your own learning, challenges, and success to bring others' awareness to their alignment with the directives. This approach will increase each individual's awareness, one of the most important aspects of coaching, and it's a freebie. There's no need for a coaching session or an identified issue with the person being coached. These small coaching and feedback moments are important in building momentum for the new directives.

Three principles will help you use feedback more effectively.

(1) Live is better than e-mail. If you are remote from the individual to whom you want to give feedback, pick up the phone. E-mail leaves too much room for misinterpretation and too little room to *connect, really*.

(2) Now is better than later. The less time that elapses between the incident and your feedback, the more powerful your feedback will be.

(3) Impact is better than intentions. Focus your feedback on the impact the individual had, not on your inferences about his intentions. The individual knows his intentions better than you do, but you have valuable data to offer about the impact he had on you and perhaps on others.

Building awareness of the directives in these ways provides new data for Tracks 2 and 3 (events and interpretations) of the Gorilla's Guide. You may also be providing material for the grapevine.

The Grapevine

The grapevine is one of the fastest, easiest ways to get information circulated in an organization. There are an amazing number of connections among the people in your organization (and beyond) that have nothing to do with lines of authority or official workflow. You can't control the grapevine, but you can seed it with your stories. Remember that stories are the main ingredient of the Gorilla's Guide. To change it, you have to get new stories circulating.

To seed the grapevine, use both your own actions and key influencers in your organization. Be sure to include both official and unofficial influencers—they are often not the same people. In the hit movie, *M*A*S*H*, Lieutenant Colonel Blake was the most powerful official influencer. Radar, however, wielded significant power. He didn't have rank and he wasn't physically imposing. But he did know how to get resources and information. That gave him power. He was a significant unofficial influencer.

If you are an influencer, official or unofficial, the Gorilla watches you closely. You might be an influencer because you are the boss, have guru status in a technical area, have access to scarce resources, or for some other reason particular to your organization. Your actions need to be consistent over time so the new messages dominate the Gorilla's Guide and shape the Gorilla's decisions about how to behave. You also need to identify other influencers who can take up the cause with you. Use them to seed the grapevine so their actions provide further momentum for the change.

The grapevine is great at carrying stories. Seed it with the stories you want by noticing successes. Tell stories about heroes of the new culture— small successes that show how great the company is with the new directives in action. Enlist other influencers to spread the stories.

Leaders often feel too rushed to tell a powerful story. They may feel their time is better spent on the facts, but studies consistently indicate that stories stick in our minds better than data. Telling a story that will cause a shift in attitudes or behaviors also requires a bit of personal vulnerability. It will often reveal the storyteller's human failings. Using details that provide context and drama, the gifted storyteller shows her authenticity, compassion, and humility. These qualities produce the most effective stories. Not every seed you plant on the grapevine has to be an emotionally powerful story. But when the opportunity arises, take advantage of it.

Remember the incident involving the computer company's failed strategy to make software a profitable business? After a couple of failed initiatives to make the strategic change, the new division general manager asked Dena, his vice president of human resources, what she thought was holding the division back. She suggested the culture might be the problem.

After a careful analysis of the Gorilla's Guide, we were able to identify specific changes that were required. By working closely with the influencers in the division, Dena and the general manager got stories of the new heroes circulating through the grapevine. Over time, we were able to modify the Gorilla's Guide and shift to a more market-focused organization. Without this change in the culture, this would have been another failed attempt to make a strategic business shift.

To get the stories on your grapevine, enlist others' help. Identify a few people who really get it—those who understand and support what you are trying to do. Ask them to be on the lookout for new heroes. When they notice a success—large or small—it's their job to spread the story on the grapevine. In the previous example, the general manager and the human resources vice president identified a few key influencers to help with this task. When they saw an instance of a developer focused on customers' needs and creating success, they found opportunities to tell other developers about it, probably at the coffeepot or in the hallway. They were seeding the grapevine and creating new heroes. Some seeds sprouted; some didn't. Enough did so that the stories spread and the Gorilla's Guide changed. The culture began to change, and the division became more market-focused.

Before communications technology became so pervasive, the grapevine was mostly person to person. Now stories can be spread on the grapevine through e-mail, blogs, social networking sites, instant messaging, and many other technologies. These technologies give the grapevine even more power. What was once spread one-to-one can now be spread one-to-many instantaneously. When Nido Qubein joined the Facebook group that was complaining about the cafeteria at High Point University, he wasn't trying to shut it down. He simply wanted to be part of the conversation. What a great way to use the informal systems and the grapevine to manage culture!

The Bottom Line

When you *second nature the behaviors* in a consistent way, your directives get built into the system; they become hardwired. *State the directives*, *be the message*, and *second nature the behaviors* are all interdependent. None of them alone will allow you to manage your culture, but all three taken together will.

Action Plan:

Second Nature the Behaviors

- Evaluate the alignment of your official systems with your directives.
- Ensure you are hiring for both job fit and culture fit.
- Provide in-the-moment coaching and feedback about alignment with your directives.
- Find stories of behavior aligned with the directives; get them on the grapevine.

CONCLUSION

STAND YOUR GROUND

A huge silverback male gorilla is screaming and charging at you, pounding his chest. Your instinct is to run, right? Fossey, however, knew that standing her ground was much less likely to result in injury than attempting to flee. In spite of that, she found that she was only able to stand her ground by clinging desperately to the vines and bushes. Otherwise, Fossey says, "I surely would have turned tail and run."

Gorillas in the Mist

When your 800-Pound Gorilla organizational culture is charging, your instinct may be to flee the scene. However, like Fossey you must stand your ground. Culture eats strategy for lunch every day. You've seen that happen all too often. Don't let it happen to you. You have the tools in your hands to turn your culture into a competitive advantage. You can do that, or you can leave it to chance. It's time to manage the fourth factor—culture—with the same skill and attention you bring to managing the other factors that are critical to your success

We've covered the directives that you need in your Gorilla's Guide and how to successfully implement them in your organization. Before we close, let's tie together the threads of three disciplines that are woven throughout this book:

- Communication
- Congruence
- Consistency

Communication

We've talked a lot about communication—the direct, explicit communication of your expectations, the way your behavior communicates your expectations, and the role of formal policies and procedures in communicating expectations. One way or the other, all of these highlight your expectations. Communication is also embedded in many of the directives:

Connect, really has communication as a central component. How can you connect without communicating?

Include respectfully reminds us that communication can serve either to include or exclude team members.

Integrate radically widens the circle of those with whom we need to communicate.

Clear, consistent, authentic communication is fundamental to managing culture. Your Gorilla is constantly communicating with your employees—you must do the same! Be vigilant about what you are communicating with both your actions and your words.

Congruence

The Latin root of congruence is "to agree." In this context, congruence means agreeing with yourself. All of your behavior must be congruent—of one mind. Because many of us don't see the inconsistencies in ourselves, you'll need feedback to keep turning up the dial on the congruence in your life. Congruence is woven throughout the directives:

Connect, really reminds us that authenticity and self-awareness are integral to leadership in managing culture.

Commit responsibly relies on congruence to ensure that commitments are strong.

Be the message is impossible without feedback and alignment, which rely heavily on your communication.

Congruence between your directives and who you are is crucial to your ability to lead a culture change effort.

Consistency

The consistent repetition of your directives and expectations is essential. This theme is woven throughout the three chapters on the actions required to manage culture:

State the directives reinforces the principle that you must communicate consistently across different media and audiences.

Be the message drills down on the consistency between who you are and what you do and say.

Second nature the behaviors teaches you how to make the operation of your systems, both informal and official, consistent with your directives.

As you work with the key behaviors in each of the directives, you'll also find an internal consistency. The behaviors for each directive support the others. It's an integrated system. That's part of the consistency that your Gorilla needs to make the shift.

Find opportunities to exercise the discipline of consistency by using the official and informal systems to ensure consistent and repeated support of the messages. Seek out and reconcile inconsistencies.

Courage

Managing culture takes courage. The courage to see your mistakes, admit them, and correct them. The courage to persist in the face of setbacks and resistance. The courage to give honest and direct feedback and accept it from others. The courage to go toe-to-toe with something that is bigger than any of us (but made up of all of us), hates change, and is invisible.

Bill O'Brien, CEO, Hanover Insurance, summed it up this way. "We didn't start out to create a culture or to be a learning organization. Our starting point was a high level of frustration at the waste of human talent. We thought that the politics, the bureaucracy, and all the bullshit was a bad environment for our people and that they were working at 30% of their mental and imaginative capabilities, quality of thinking, and spirit."

Regardless of whether you are the CEO, a manager, or an informal leader, managing the culture of your organization takes courage. If you back up your courage with communication, consistency, and congruence, you can manage your culture. It will take a sustained effort over time to make a difference, especially in a large organization. During that time, you will be proactively managing your culture—the fourth factor. In doing that, you will have discovered an important lever for your success.

REFERENCES

Borton, Terry. *Reach, Touch and Teach*. New York: McGraw-Hill, 1970.

Cook Ross, Inc. *Cultural Communication Guide*. www.CookRoss.com, 2006.

de Geus, Arie. *The Living Company*. Boston: Harvard Business School Press, 1997.

Fiorina, Carly. *Tough Choices*. New York: Penguin Group, 2006.

Fossey, Dian. *Gorillas in the Mist*. Boston: Houghton Mifflin, 1983.

Foxman, Joel, and Robert Radtke. 1970. Negative Expectancy and the Choice of an Aversive Task. *Journal of Personality and Social Psychology*. 15: 253–257.

Gomes, Lee. 2006. Above All Else, Rivals of Apple Mostly Need Some Design Mojo. *Wall Street Journal*, May 24, Marketplace section.

Halkias, Maria. Penney remakes culture to remake image. *Dallas Morning News*, February 11.

Harvey, Jerry. 1974. The Abilene Paradox: The Management of Agreement. *Organizational Dynamics*.

Inskeep, Steve. 2006. Amid missteps, some question Microsoft resilience. *NPR Morning Edition*, June 19.

Karlgaard, Rich. 2005. Carly Fiorina's Seven Deadly Sins. *Wall Street Journal,* February 11, Eastern Edition.

Kegan, Robert, and Lisa Lahey. *How the Way We Talk Can Change the Way We Work*. San Francisco: Jossey-Bass, 2001.

Kleiner, Art. *Who Really Matters: The Core Group Theory of Power, Privilege, and Success*. New York: Doubleday, 2003.

Lynch, Larry. 2001. Sustaining Innovation: Walt Disney instilled how. *T+D*, 55: 44–49.

Pink, Daniel. *A Whole New Mind*. New York: Riverhead Books, 2005.

Powers, Lauren. *The Trouble with Thinking: the Dangerous Trip from In the Head to Out the Mouth*. New York: iUniverse, 2006.

Senge, Peter, Art Kleiner, Charlotte Roberts, Richard Ross, and Bryan
    Smith. *The Fifth Discipline Fieldbook: Strategies and Tools for Build-
    ing a Learning Organization*. New York: Doubleday, 1994

Sugarman, Barry. 2001. Twenty Years of Organizational Learning and
    Ethics at Hanover Insurance: Interviews with Bill O'Brien. *Reflections*
    3:7–17.

Zades, Stephen, and Jane Stephens. *Mad Dogs, Dreamers and Sages*.
    Elounda Press, 2003.

ABOUT THE AUTHOR

By revealing the invisible patterns in their organizations, Dr. Linda Ford has shown hundreds of executives how to successfully drive organizational performance. Linda is committed to helping senior executives manage the fourth factor — culture. She consults and speaks on improving business performance.

After earning her undergraduate degree in mathematics, Linda spent fourteen years in large global corporations working in almost every function in the company. She has been successful in field sales, software development, product management, marketing, and line management. She earned her PhD in Human and Organization Systems from the Fielding Graduate University in 1992.

Most recently, in fifteen years of consulting work, Linda has worked with organizations to achieve performance outcomes such as:

- Saving millions of dollars in inventory costs
- Turning a cost center to a profit center
- Reducing time to market for new products

And, she raised two teenagers as a single mom and lived to tell the tale! After twenty-five years in Silicon Valley, Linda is back home in Texas. She lives in Austin with her cat, Lizzie.

To learn more about how Linda can help your organization be more successful, visit www.FordBusinessConsulting.com.

CPSIA information can be obtained at www.ICGtesting.com
Printed in the USA
LVOW010416130413

328884LV00003B/361/A